The Choice for Consciousness
Tools for Conscious Living
Volume 1

The Choice for Consciousness

Tools for Conscious Living

Volume 1

✦✦✦

Eloheim and The Council

Channeled by
Veronica Torres

Second edition January 2012
This edition contains updated tools and terms

ISBN: 978-1-936969-17-3

Copyright 2011 Veronica Torres
Eloheim.com

Published by Rontor Presents

Cover Art by Holly's Creative Design
Hollyscreative.com

Interior Design by Mary T. George
Epubpub.com

Acknowledgements

When I say this book would not have been possible without the help of the following people, I truly mean it. I have tried for five years to produce a book of the Eloheim teachings. It is only now, with this amazing group of people in my life, that it has become possible.

Sue Trainor transcribed two years of Eloheim and The Council meetings; nearly one million words. Yes, one million. I have never felt as abundant as when I received her email offering to transcribe the Eloheim sessions. This book was born in that moment.

Mary Ricci edited every one of those million words. Eloheim has a lot to say and Mary somehow manages to get the nuances, looks, body language, and general Eloheim vibe to show up in the written form. As I don't always remember the channeling, reading the transcript often feels like the first time I am experiencing the material. I am so grateful for this gift.

Waller Jamison has contributed to many of my projects, a lot of which are still in progress. I am so grateful for her help with the overview in this volume. Plus, she makes me laugh until I can't breathe every time I talk to her. A rare ability.

Mary T. George keeps the computers running, manages the technological aspects of the webcasts and recordings, and creates fabulous PowerPoint presentations, but I learned her true super-hero power when she was able to distill the one-million-word transcript into manageable sections. But, that's not all, she also managed to convert and format the book so that it can be read on a variety of e-readers and other devices. Now she is doing the interior formatting for the print editions. WOW. I mean it. WOW!

Margy Henderson proves that you can choose your family, it just might take a while to find them. She may not be my biological mother, but her unwavering support makes her the best Mom I could imagine. She loves me and entertains me in equal measure. Plus, sometimes she calls just to remind me that I am perfect. How cool is that?

Peter Lambertson has the unique ability to kick me in the pants without ever making it seem like I just got my ass kicked. He was the tipping point to getting this book into form, and he is an amazing friend.

I also want to thank the hundreds of people who have attended Eloheim sessions over the past nine years. Without their willingness and openness none of this would have ever happened. I specifically want to thank Randy Sue Collins, who I am certain has driven me more miles in the last five years than I have driven myself; John Murray, who opened his home to our group and is always ready with solid advice; and Richard Applegate, who is a master of the intricacies of Microsoft Word and a great support in many ways.

Thank you all so very, very much.
Veronica
February 2011

Living from the soul's perspective, of course,
is only achievable
by Being in the Moment.

Being in the Moment is really only achievable
by not having baggage with you in the Moment.

Not having baggage in the Moment is only achievable
by becoming conscious of your baggage.

Becoming conscious of what's going on in the moment is only
possible if you're willing to break habits.

Breaking habits is only possible if you're willing to confront the
biology that says, "Change is too scary."

Confronting the biology is only possible if you have courage.
So it starts with the courage to say, "Life can be different."

Once you can say that, then you confront the biology,
you become conscious,
you start seeing where your baggage is,
you release your baggage,
you are in the moment.

And because by then your vibration is so high,
the Moment allows you access to your soul,
to the Akashic Records,
and to a completely different way of living which is:

Being in the body, but living from your soul's perspective.

—*Eloheim*

Contents

Introduction

Why would you want to make the choice for consciousness? What are tools for conscious living?

Two very important questions.

Here are four more: Are you living in peace? Are you living in joy? Are you living in serenity? Are you living in bliss?

And, the most important question: Are you ready to take bold steps in that direction?

Moving out of a fear-based operating system into a consciousness-based operating system allows you to experience being human in a brand-new way. A way that isn't driven by habit, repetitive thinking, reliving the past, speculating about the future, or being paralyzed by the fear of change.

It is a way of living that focuses on an authentic experience of the moment, awareness of your truth, and the full comprehension that by choosing your reaction to every one of your experiences, you are creating your reality.

In this volume, and the others that will follow, we will introduce many simple but powerful tools that will help you make the shift from the fear-based operating system (survival) to the consciousness-based operating system (fascination). The tools can be used throughout your spiritual journey. They require no props, no rituals, no religious beliefs, and can be easily incorporated into your day-to-day activities. In addition, they build on each other and can be used in powerful combinations that will rapidly transform your experience.

The first section of this volume introduces 22 of our tools. The second section defines and clarifies 126 terms and concepts. You can read this volume in any order. It is not a narrative, but a reference book we hope you will turn to time and time again.

Later volumes will introduce additional tools. These tools were created during our public and private sessions in response to questions posed to us.

Each tool is followed by comments from folks who have been using them. Their insights and examples will provide additional ways that the tools can be applied.

In the appendix, you can read more about us, learn how we came to work with Veronica, and find out how to become involved in our meetings.

We are very pleased to have the opportunity to connect with you.

—*Eloheim*

Overview

Before we open the toolbox, we'd like to clarify some important terms.

First, we have to define the concept of "you." You are an infinite, immortal soul. Souls are fascinated by EVERYTHING and want to have a huge and diverse set of experiences. One of the things your soul wants to experience is what it is like to live here on Earth.

Living on Earth is very different from how you live as a soul. As a soul, you know that you are one with all; as a human, you often feel completely separate and alone. As a soul, you know that every experience is fascinating and educational; as a human you judge most things as right or wrong, good or bad. As a soul, you know you stand outside of time and will have every opportunity for any experience you wish to have; as a human, you are convinced that scarcity and lack are your constant companions.

Why would a soul want to experience Earth? Why would a soul do something that is so challenging? The simple answer is this: Because it is fascinating.

You don't believe us? You, as a human, do exactly the same thing.

You have a game called Pin the Tail on the Donkey, which illustrates how, even in a simple child's game, you take something incredibly easy and make it more difficult on purpose. The aim of the game is to pin a paper tail on a paper donkey and the person who sticks it closest to where you would find a real tail on a real donkey is the winner. How hard can that be? Apparently, not hard enough! First, you are blindfolded. Then, someone spins you around and around and points you in approximately the right direction. You then stumble and bumble toward your target and everyone gets a great laugh from your attempt to pin the tail in the right place. Your fun is increased by the addition of the blindfold and the dizziness. This is a perfect example of how you make things harder, on purpose, because the added challenge gives you more opportunities to be fascinated.

Let's also explore the idea of the moment. The moment isn't a place that you find yourself in very often. Your attention is constantly being pulled into the past or projected into the future. However, living in the moment—the actual experience of now without the influence of the past or the future—is a crucial aspect of living from the consciousness-based operating system.

Here is a fun way to visualize this idea: Let's say you are visiting an amusement park and you know that you will be leaving at 5 P.M. Do you arrive at 9 A.M. and go to the exit to wait for 5 P.M., just to be certain you will leave on time? Of course not! You are there to experience the rides, to take photos with people in large costumes, and to do all the other things that you enjoy so much. It's the same with life—you are not here for the conclusion. When you live in the past or the future, it is just like waiting at the exit all day, you are not where the action is taking place.

Transforming your relationship to the moment is one of the key elements of living a conscious life. Our tools are specifically designed to help you change your habitual fear of the moment into an opportunity to be fascinated by the moment.

Sometimes people will say to us, "Sure, I want my life to change, but it's so hard!" We'd like to remind you that you choose to do hard things all of time. You like to learn new languages and to play musical instruments and some of you even enjoy climbing Mount Everest. All of these are pretty challenging, yet you choose to do them and you even expect them to be hard. But when it comes to challenges on your spiritual path, you tend to see "hard" as meaning you are a victim.

You are not a victim unless you choose to be one. This is a very important distinction. We have many tools to support you in the choice to experience yourself as a creator. You are creating everything that is going on in your life, including the things that you would describe as negative, bad, painful, or even wrong. If you think you aren't creating your life, you are mistaken—this is one of the few certainties we can point out to you. You are creating your life in every moment. You are creating it through your *reactions* to your experiences. The tools in this book will help you become more comfortable with this concept and how to use them to leave the fear-based operating system.

Lastly, we want to address your relationship to fear. Fear is an intrinsic part of the human condition; you have it programmed into your DNA, in the form of the survival instinct. You might think of the survival instinct being focused on only keeping you alive, but fear and the survival instinct also express in such ways as worry about money, anxiety about your relationships, insecurity about jobs, and concerns about your children. Evolving your relationship to the survival instinct is one of the key components of living from the consciousness-based operating system.

Remember that very little in your life changes externally before you change internally. It is the internal changes in attitude, habits, and relationships to fears and triggers that generate the external changes you want to see in your life.

Let's open the tool box and explore together!

Tools

Candle wax (Nobody gets your wax)

This tool is based in an analogy: You are a candle. You can share your flame—your emanation—but you cannot give away your wax. Never, never, never, never. If you give away your wax, you give away yourself, and who you are is diminished.

If you're a candle, you can light numerous other candles with your flame, but nobody gets your wax. On some level, we see you energetically very drained because your wax has not been precious to you. That core amount of attention, of rest, of nourishment, of peace, of quiet, of meditation, of walking, dancing, whatever it is that you know feeds you as a person and keeps you whole. You've been letting pieces of those things go to other people because you thought, "Well, if they're happy, I'll be happy." Or, "If they're happy, at least I won't be so distracted by their needs." When the truth is, you've gotten yourself drained and you'll get further drained. So, step back and set boundaries. Boundaries don't mean: "I don't love you anymore." Boundaries mean: "I have to love myself first, so I have extra love to give. I can't give from this place. I have to give from a whole place." If you keep giving from weakness, eventually you have nothing left, but if you set boundaries, you rejuvenate yourself.

The first step is to set boundaries so that the people you're giving your wax to don't get any more. And they usually throw fits, so you have to deal with that. They'll call you selfish, typically. Or they'll call you a bitch.

When you drop service mentality and take care of yourself first, you're able to offer something extraordinary. It's the candle. The candle is lit and the flame is giving off light. It gives off light whether you hide it in a closet or you set it on your windowsill. And when you love yourself well, it's like putting the candle on the windowsill so the people who are driving by see the light as well.

You can give your flame to anyone because it still burns even when you share it with others, but when you start giving your wax away it's all over.

***

Veronica writes:

This was one of the early tools and it is still very much in use. It is so very easy to get pulled into "service" and siphon off your wax. I know what that feels like and I am not going back there! It is such a joy to focus on emanating my truth and knowing that that is all the "service" I need to do.

***

Habitual response of codependency felt seamless until I heard this tool. My sense of global responsibility burdened me in a way I thought was my identity as a "responsible person." I felt guilty about not being able to help all women feel safe, for instance. Imagining myself as a being who has limited physical shape (the candle as my body) with unlimited consciousness and intention (the flame), I saw immediately that the love and attention I choose to offer a situation flows from a source that is constantly renewable. When I have used as much of my physical energy to support my intentions as I have available, I must rest without shame. Actually, to rest with relish, enjoying the dreams that replenish insights and creativity.

—*Margy Henderson*

***

The candle wax tool is very good for me as I have a tendency to go out of my way to help others, sometimes to great lengths. So, the idea of sharing my flame and not my wax made very good sense to me. It's helping me to be crystal clear on when I may be stepping over the line and when I need to reel it back in.

—Joseph

Choose and choose again

The transition from the fear-based operating system to the consciousness-based operating system is not done in a straight line. You must choose and choose again for transformation. Habit is very strong, the survival instinct runs very deep, cultural and DNA pressures are intense—your choice to grow spiritually requires spiritual discipline and persistence. It is an act of committing and re-committing to the journey.

Remember: Fear is a choice, not a mandate.

***

Veronica writes:

A reminder tool. Sort of like a condiment. Use frequently. Use liberally. Always have it around.

Clarity vs. certainty

You are programmed in the fear-based operating system to look for certainty. Certainty says, "I'm not going to risk any change unless I know ahead of time how it's going to work out."

Certainty is a fallacy; it is actually impossible to be certain of anything, but the habit of seeking it runs very deep.

Clarity is the opportunity to experience insight. Clarity is only accessible in the moment. It does not come from the thinking mind, but is inspiration received by connecting with your soul's perspective.

Clarity is, "Oh, yeah, that's a good idea," without having any connection to the outcome of using that idea. Certainty is, "I will not act unless I know how it's going to turn out. I'm not going to leave this marriage, I'm not going to leave this job, I'm not going to move from this apartment, unless I know where the next man is going to come from, where the next job is going to be, and where the next house is going to be. I won't leave until I know. I won't change until I know. I can't make a difference in my life until I know how it's going to be." That's certainty. Clarity is, "This relationship doesn't work for me." See how it's just so much calmer? "This relationship doesn't work for me. I don't have to know what the next relationship is going to be in order to act on the fact that this one doesn't work anymore." That's clarity. And the beauty of clarity is, clarity leads to clarity. Certainty stops. Certainty is contracting. Clarity is expanding. Clarity says, "Here is insight." Certainty says, "Until I know, I'm not going to go".

It's so much more fun to live from clarity because it always opens, opens, opens. Certainty just closes doors. When you follow clarity, it opens up more opportunities; when you wait for certainty, you can wait a really long, miserable time. In fact, you'll wait forever.

At times, the cry for certainty can be very loud; however, it is quite fascinating to see how often you are willing to operate in clarity without realizing it.

Let's say you want to go to the park for a walk. You don't know who you're going to run into, but it doesn't forestall you from going for a walk. You don't know if you're going to be warm or cold, you don't know if you're going to have the right clothes to deal with the weather. It could start raining and you don't have a raincoat. That level of uncertainty you are okay with. "Wear layers, it'll work out. Bring an umbrella, don't bring an umbrella, who cares?" Yeah, you might run into somebody, you might not.

You can do all that and not have to contend with certainty's cry for attention. However, when you get into the relationship realms, "I don't know how she feels about me," "I don't know how he feels about me," "Is he going to want to stay married to me," "Is my kid going to do well in school today?" All of a sudden, certainty is back in charge.

Notice the temptation, return to the moment, ask for clarity.

***

Veronica writes:

This one took a while to sink in for me. I was confused about how to let go of certainty when clarity felt so elusive. However, when I finally re-alized that certainty was actually elusive and clarity was real, it really was quite a transformation.

***

My two favorite tools are "I don't know anything" and "Clarity vs. certainty." These tools have helped me by turning off "mind chatter" and not needing to have security in all things and choosing clarity over certainty has helped. I am less concerned now about survival needs and requirements but feel for sure that clarity and potentials offer me a greater sense of freedom and peace vs. having to have security at all times before I act.

—J.R., Ontario, Canada

***

How often this comes up! Certainty now has a visceral "tag" for me. It feels tense, as if I'm boxed tightly all around my body when I'm trying to figure something out. I recall "clarity" and relax into a spacious listening posture. Clarity's point of reference is right now—open and available to anything new. Insight, seeing into the "clear bead at the center" wherein lies all possibility.

This makes "not knowing" a curious adventure instead of scary. I no longer expect myself to figure things out with my admittedly fine mind. I do expect that my mind will find the words to express what I gain from my insights and when I sense the authentic truth of my heart. A relaxed mind that observes my current reality has more access to intelligent and creative self-expression.

—Margy Henderson

Concurrent and cascading fears

There are two different patterns that fears follow in response to triggers.

With cascading fears, the trigger is followed by a train of fears that are similar. A classic example is when somebody cuts you off on the freeway. You react with, "Didn't he see me?" Then the train of cascading fears starts to form. You might next move to the pain you felt when you were "not seen" and passed over for promotion, then to the suffering you experienced when you were "not seen" and not invited to the prom. Before you are even aware of it, you're reliving being five years old and upset because someone took your wagon because they "didn't see you" playing with it.

Cascading fears connect experiences in the present to experiences scattered throughout your history. Not only does this result in you suffering over and over again, but it also doesn't allow you to attend to what the initial trigger was. During this cascading fear pattern, you may hear the voice of an authority figure from your childhood narrating the entire sequence. That is a way to alert yourself to the pattern.

You tend to have "favorite" cascading fear patterns that you turn to even if the initial triggers are quite varied. When you catch yourself in this fear pattern, gently remind yourself to come back to the moment, choose to stay in the moment, and allow yourself to become more conscious about your reaction to the initial trigger.

In the case of concurrent fears, the trigger is followed by a train of fears on completely different subjects, each of the fears pertaining to your current experiences rather than going into past experiences.

This pattern is typically used when you are dealing with the top triggers: Money, sex, job, housing, relationships, health. You find yourself triggered by one of these and rather than becoming conscious of the trigger and using it for your growth, you jump to the next subject. You take the triggered state with you and find something to be triggered about with the next subject.

This jumping from subject to subject and trigger to trigger is full of suffering. It makes it very difficult to actually transform any one situation. You never stay with it long enough to change it. Concurrent fears can leave you feeling like your life is full of problems and you are unable to cope with any of them.

As an example of concurrent fears, let's say you're worried about your marriage. Thinking about your marriage is too triggering, so you jump to thinking about your job. You think about your job until that is too triggering, then you jump to worrying about your heath, and on it goes. Nothing ever changes. Even the thoughts you have about each of these subjects are unchanging. You simply use the hamster-wheel mind to continue to run in circles. Suffering is the result.

The key is to pick one subject and stick with it long enough to bring consciousness to it. The pattern will try to draw you away from that one subject, but choose and choose again to stick with it, past the discomfort you are feeling.

You are looking for new information, but new information doesn't come from rehashing old thoughts, it comes from insight. When you apply consciousness to one subject you can actually be in the moment with it long enough to get to the "aha."

***

Veronica writes:

I think this tool gets the award for the tool with the most awkward name. We never did come up with a more clever way to say it. This one is really helpful in alerting you to patterns of habitual fears. I don't know how many times I have done that: trigger in the moment and all of a sudden I'm five again. Being aware of these patterns really helped me change them.

***

For me, this tool combines well with the "What is true now?" tool. When I find myself spinning off into the past or projecting into the future, I can stop myself short if I just remind myself that what is true now has nothing to do with either the past or the future. It's especially obvious to me when I'm worried about money and just switch over to worrying about my health, with no break in between! I'll know that these concurrent fears are just my hamster-wheel thinking taking me out of the moment, where my conscious self would actually rather be.

—Claire

Don't be mean to yourself (Four-year-old child)

If there's something you genuinely want to change about yourself, you don't have to be mean to yourself in order to change it. Take a moment and let that sink in. You don't have to be mean to yourself to change.

You don't berate at a child about learning to walk, or talk, or write. You say, "Hey, it's OK, let's try it again."

Yet, you will be extremely critical of yourself at nearly any opportunity.

How do you know if you are being mean to yourself? If you're talking to yourself in a voice that you wouldn't use with a four-year-old child, especially somebody else's four-year-old child, you're being mean to yourself.

When you find yourself being hard on you, simply ask yourself, "Would I say this to a pre-schooler?"

No, you would not.

It's OK to have a new plan or to desire something different for the future or to reevaluate how you handled a situation, that's all growth. But beating yourself up is so contrary to everything we teach that we have made it our only rule: You don't get to be mean to yourself.

Oh, and be aware that someday soon we are going to evolve this tool. Someday soon, we are going to lower the age. It will be, "You can't say anything to yourself that you wouldn't say to a toddler or an infant." Since you can be fascinated by EVERYTHING an infant does (Oh look, it's a poo poo!), you can, eventually, be fascinated by anything YOU do, as well. Imagine that!

***

Veronica writes:

When Eloheim says, "We only have one rule: You don't get to be mean to yourself," they really mean it! The seriousness and attention they pay to this concept is above any other.

***

I have found that this tool of "don't be mean to yourself" represents a lot of change for me! It means letting go of a lot of people who, if I am truthful with myself, no longer fit in my life. Being nice to myself, ultimately, means being willing to be available for new people entirely, by being willing to be alone first. It's somewhat sad but also liberating to be in my truth in this way.

 —Anne Marie

***

Just last night, I was talking with my friend—he was sitting on the edge of my big overstuffed brown couch. I was on the opposite sofa looking past him for a way out of a conversation that was spiraling down into argument-land. "Don't be mean to me" popped in and in that instant, we softened our stance. Our outcome also magically changed.

Experiencing the words "don't be mean to me" feels like folding my legs and falling into soft ground with my arms around the neck of a lovely, beautiful beast.

"Don't be mean to me" is my "fallback" tool. It wins every argument. It connects with everyone's heart, so everyone gets it.

 —Denise

***

I used to berate myself internally all the time until I started practicing this tool. I would catch myself as soon as I started to hear the negative chatter, and have been able to transform that nasty voice into a loving, supportive, helpful voice for me now!

—*Randy Sue Collins*

Don't put handcuffs on God

This tool is a shortcut with a funny image to help you remember this concept: don't limit your current experience by deciding ahead of time what is possible or what is impossible.

"Don't put handcuffs on God," is the same thing as saying, "Is what you believe is currently possible based only on what the past has shown you or are you allowing new possibilities to exist within you?"

***

Question: I have been experiencing intense fatigue. I have been asking my guides, angels, my own soul for hits on what I can do energetically and physically to optimize the experience.

Eloheim: It's perfectly fine to ask for support. Just be cautious saying, "Okay, I feel this fatigue, so I want my soul to come in and make it go back to the way it used to be. I want to have all that energy again." Or, "I want to feel the way I used to feel." Be really cautious about "I want to feel the way I used to feel." It's better as you said, "I want to optimize this experience, I want to flow through it, I want to remove any blocks, I want to get to the other side of this with as much ease as possible." But don't put handcuffs on God about what the other side of it is, because you've never experienced it. We don't want you to limit the possibilities that you have open to you by deciding ahead of time that a certain amount of energy or feeling a certain way or sleeping a certain number of hours is the answer for you because the answer is an expanded awareness of what's newly possible.

***

Veronica writes:

I get triggered by this tool. I always wonder if people will see the word "God" and have an issue with it. Then I picture God wearing the handcuffs that I put on him/her/it and I just laugh. Handcuffs on creation? Handcuffs on limitless potential? Handcuffs on universal energy? Pretty funny image, whatever word you use.

***

This tool enables me to stop my mind from trying to figure out "how" I'm going to do or get something and stay in the space of "what" I want, which allows for my soul's voice to be heard.

—Randy Sue Collins

***

I have a belief that I do not have enough money to move. I stay in the box of that belief, which makes me feel very tired. I do not reach out for employment opportunity.

I decided to trust that moving is a dandy notion, and someone called me to do a care-giving job for six weeks and now I have enough money to move. Then, I decided to get dentistry done, which I'd been procrastinating about and actually need more than moving. Now, I notice that I like where I am living, which surprises me. No handcuffs. Flow in possibility.

—Margy Henderson

***

During the protests in Tahrir Square in Cairo I was tempted many times to engage in discussions on Facebook and at work about the demonstrations and what might happen both in day-to-day confrontations and eventual outcomes. I struggled to stay neutral in my observation and to avoid cynical or overly hopeful and idealistic thoughts. I felt deeply that to do otherwise would be to put handcuffs on God. I just kept saying "Let the outcome be one that will promote healing above all else."

—Rene

How ridiculous does it have it get?

How ridiculous does it have to get before you are willing to change a habit? How much suffering must you experience? How many times do you have to experience the same patterns?

How ridiculous does it have to get? The answer? Usually, pretty damned ridiculous.

You're constantly putting up barrier after barrier after barrier to taking responsibility for your creation because the habit of victimhood is so strong in you. Sure, the choice for consciousness is challenging, but suffering is painful and repetitive. Owning "I did this" might be hard, but what is the alternative?

Don't require it to become ridiculous before you are willing to transform it. If it has become ridiculous, then transform it immediately!

***

Veronica writes:

When it gets ridiculous, I KNOW whatever it is must move to the top of my to-do list. I must stop and become as conscious as possible about what is going on and what I am experiencing. When it is ridiculous, I bust out all the tools until it isn't ridiculous anymore!

***

I remember this tool when I notice things building to a frenzy and chaos begins to reign. It reminds me to get conscious quick—and often leads to a bout of laughter!

—Randy Sue Collins

***

How ridiculous does it have to get? This tool is actually somewhat soothing for me. Living in a foreign country with a busy schedule and acclimating to new standards and rules, many interesting and exasperating scenarios pop up daily. At one point, I was writing them all down because I didn't know what to do with them and all the emotional responses that were getting triggered. With this tool, I can be amused. I can laugh more. And it helps me focus on what I get to look at—on why this is happening FOR me, or what is the VELCRO here, who is answering the door, why this is in my lap—it is a personal inner adventure more than an external chronicle of events.

—Anna R., Mexico

I don't know anything

You really do not know ANYTHING, and this should please you. You don't know anything about this moment because you have never been in it before. You are brand-new here.

Your human life has been one of limitation. Spiritual growth is all about transformation and expansion. As you move along your spiritual journey, you move into brand-new territory, territory you truly don't know anything about.

You have the opportunity here to say, "I don't know anything. I only know about limitation and I'm not satisfied only knowing limitation. I am ready to live an expanded experience, and in order to do so I have to acknowledge I don't know a darn thing about living in an expanded way." Because you don't. You absolutely do not know a thing about living an expanded life.

What you're saying is, "I don't know anything about what's going on. I don't have an opinion about it. I don't have a judgment about it. I don't have any insight about it other than the insight I open up to."

The first step whenever you're trying to open up to a new possibility is to say, "I don't know anything in this moment about this." You've never been in this moment asking this question before. So, that's not a lie. That's not a crutch. That's not a coping mechanism.

It is the truth. And truth immediately puts you into a higher-vibrational state, which makes accessing further insight easier and easier.

Stay open with: "I don't know anything about now, but I know what I bring to now." You don't come into the now as a babe fresh out of the womb. You come into the now with the collection of yourself, and the best you can do is to be in the now with an open and receptive position that allows you to evaluate and interact with the experience as it unfolds.

By saying "I don't know how to do it," or "I don't know anything about it," that becomes the truth, it clears the decks, it sort of starts you over. And it starts you over where? Right here. Not back to the beginning, but right here and now. So, "I don't know anything about it."

Immediately after "I don't know anything," comes "Am I bringing the past or the future into this moment?" That is your habit. "I don't know, but I have to look for an answer." Monitor yourself for the past creeping in to say, "It's never worked before, I've been trying so hard." Or the future popping up.

If the past and future shows up, return to "I don't know anything." Don't allow the habit of leaving the moment to run the show.

Let go of preconceived notions. Let go of future projections. Allow in the expansiveness that you have never ever experienced before. This is the good stuff.

And remember that there's a lot of fascination in every moment, especially when you don't decide you know what's going on. So "What is true now?" may get you into that peaceful state and then it's, "I don't know anything about this peaceful state," because you don't want to project old patterns into the truth of you. You want to explore the truth of you and being able to say "I don't know anything about this" helps keep you from bringing old baggage into that new moment.

When we first gave you the "I don't know anything" tool, we were met with a lot of resistance. The resistance came because you have big brains and you're super-smart, and when we said, "You don't know anything," you all went: "Arrgghh! Yes, I do know something."

Eventually, the response changed to: "Wow, that's the biggest help I've ever had—to not have to always feel like I'm on the hook to know everything."

***

Veronica writes:

Oh, this one made people MAD! I got so many emails saying, "What do they mean, I don't know anything?!" Probably because I was saying the same thing to myself! We are so accustomed to being judged by our knowledge. When this tool clicked for me, it was a gate latch that sounded like a sonic boom. You mean, I don't HAVE to know everything to feel safe? You mean, I can just be? A revolutionary idea.

***

My ego did not like this tool at first, but using it over and over let me off the hook of needing an answer for anything. Ego out of the way lets Soul's perspective come through.

—Randy Sue Collins

***

"I don't know anything" clearly shows me how I make assumptions and draw conclusions on subjects of which I have no knowledge.

—Mike

***

My favorite tool, "I don't know anything," is subtle yet intensely profound. When its meaning is truly grasped there is great comfort in knowing you really don't know anything. Ironically, this may not be a popular concept in spiritual circles as many aspirants I've come across think they "know everything."

—John M.

Neutral observation

A tool that says, "I'm not going to take my habitual response as the mandated action." It means, "I'm going to stop and ask what is actually going on here in this moment."

Neutral observation is like carving out a little space that says, "In this moment, instead of all the habitual ways I could react, I'm going to open to hearing a new way, open to insight from my soul, and ask, 'What is this teaching me?' and, 'What am I learning?' to carve out a space where my reaction can be something new rather than habitual."

Neutrality doesn't have duality in it. Neutrality doesn't have judgments in it. Neutrality doesn't have all these places within you that you have habitually gone with situations. That's one of the reasons that it's hard to go into neutral observation, because you have all these little niches in you where your habits runs. Habit takes you here, habit takes you there, and you're just thinking, "How can I be neutral in this moment?" Well, it takes a little practice. You're literally rewiring your neural pathways in order for this to work.

So, let's say you have insecurity about a project, "Oh, I have this project and I don't know how it's going to turn out." If you're in the fear, then it's "I don't know what's going to happen," and you start hamster-wheel thinking, "I should do this, maybe I should do this, maybe I shouldn't have started this." Everybody knows what that feels like. If we take that up into a higher-vibration space, it's "Wow, there's that feeling in my chest again, interesting, it's showing up again. There's that feeling of 'there's potential for failure here.' Wow, failure is a judgment. The truth is, everything's a learning experience. If I can look at this neutrally, then the outcome isn't what drives this experience. This fear is based on a need for a certain outcome. These feelings in my body are being elicited by a need for a certain outcome. If I can see this neutrally and just say 'Wow, there's that fear, there's that habit popping up again, I can feel it in my chest, I see it in my life, but I'm not attached to the outcome that that fear is trying to get me to attach to'."

The fear is saying, "The shit's hitting the fan." Neutral observation says, "Everything's interesting." When you can stay neutral, you can feel the fear but say, "I'm just going to see it. I'm not going to let the feeling of the fear tell me what to do next, I'm going to let neutral observation and insight from my soul reveal what's going to happen next, and every time that fear stirs up in me, I'm going to make another choice for insight. I'm going to make another choice just to watch it rather than let it drive the experience I'm in." And that, of course, takes a little bit of practice but those neural pathways will lay down very quickly because it's a high-vibrational activity and because it actually leads to so much relief of the body's tension.

When you can sit in neutral observation and say, "I see the body reacting but that's not the choice I'm making", the body starts to calm. You "calm" into a higher vibration rather than "stir up" in a lower vibration. And that's really the cusp of this whole thing. Watch the fear, knowing it's an option and not a mandate. Choose again and again to see it, rather than be it. Even if you feel it, still say, "I see you, fear. I feel you trying to show up in my life and run the show but I'm not going on that path. I'm not attached to the outcome you're trying to scare me about. I'm going to sit here and I'm going to be as neutral as possible and point you out to myself," and the fears will dissipate. They have to. Because when you take something that's low-vibration and infuse it with high-vibration, it can't last. It's like putting an ice cube in a microwave. It can't last. Biologically incompatible. It can't last in that environment.

Neutral observation is not numb. Neutral observation is being extremely aware of what is going on and choosing to have as neutral as possible experience of it.

Neutral observation doesn't make you a doormat. In fact, neutral observation only works when you set boundaries.

***

Eloheim: Neutral observation stops in the moment, collects what the moment is offering, sets boundaries, and then moves into, "Where's the aha, where's the learning, where's the next step here?" and then into action, which leads to a new moment, which leads to an opportunity for neutral observation.

Response: Which is so hard.

Eloheim: We understand. But we also see very clearly that when you live in habitual response, it's painful. Neutral observation is challenging but habitual response is painful.

Response: Where's the switch to turn it on and off?

Eloheim: It's really spiritual choice. It's that choice that says, "I know I'm in habit. I know I'm in a coping mechanism. I know I'm using fear. I know I'm bringing the past or the future into this moment." It's just catching yourself and then saying to yourself, "I know where this leads." It's like when you have a bad breakup and you're listening to a sad song on the radio and you have your hand on the phone and you're gonna call. You're gonna call that person that just broke up with you and you know, you have your hand on the phone and you know, what's going to happen when you dial that phone. You know it's going to be ugly. You know they don't want to hear from you. You know that you're going to hear stuff that you don't want to hear; even if you get the answering machine, you don't want to hear the answering machine, you don't even know what you want from the person, you just know that that's what you think is your coping mechanism. That pain on the other side of the phone.

Now, to let go of the phone, to be conscious—to sit with that is very challenging and it can be emotional, but you know what happens if you pick up the phone, so you have a choice. And the choice is to be disciplined enough to say that the habit of picking up the phone is less attractive than the challenge of becoming conscious in this moment.

Neutral observation doesn't mean numb. Neutral observation means, "I don't know everything, therefore I'm going to open to my soul helping me see all that I can so that I choose, state preferences, and set boundaries in order to operate from the most grace, ease, and bliss possible in this dynamic." And that can be applied to every single moment.

***

Veronica writes:

Oh yes, Neutral observation, my old friend. This was one of the first tools Eloheim ever gave us. It feels like putting on a comfortable pair of jeans or my favorite boots. Relaxing into an alternative to the hamster-wheel mind and the requirement to know everything.

***

To me, Neutral observation is one of the most important and useful tools of all. When I am in neutral observation, I immediately go into the present moment and I become aware, at a gut level, that my thinking mind holds a gentle tyranny over me. If I'm not very aware, it runs my life through habitual patterns and knee-jerk reactions. This practice has also made me aware that there is room for very little or no spontaneous action on my part when the habitual mind is in control. I live much more cleanly and peacefully when I can remember to stay in Neutral observation.

—Janice Imbach

***

This tool helps me step back and not take things so damn seriously. Allows the bigger picture to be seen.

—Randy Sue Collins

***

Neutral observation stops me from becoming overly emotional when I am triggered. I find myself in a space where time seems to stand still and provides an opportunity for me to view my situation and its many options.

—Donna Price

"No" is a complete sentence / Say "no" first

This tool allows you to set a boundary or state a preference without feeling the need to justify or make excuses for your position. You are not responsible for others' reactions to your choices. Stating a preference is an act of free will.

A fascinating way to learn about boundaries, preferences, and "What is true now?" is to say "no" first. Just give it a try! Someone calls you up and asks you to go out. Say "no" first.

If you are habitually saying "yes" to keep other people happy, try saying "no" and see how it makes you feel. The result we have seen is that being able to just say no is incredibly liberating. Importantly, it gives you the time to actually find out how you feel. When you say no first, you can then consider your feelings on the matter without the pressure of having the question hanging over your head.

If you decide that you actually do want to participate—because YOU want to, not just to make another happy—you can always call back and say you changed your mind.

And "No, period" is a complete sentence. You don't have to explain. There is no need for a lie, an excuse, or even other plans. If you are asked, "Why?" you can just say, "It's just not right for me."

If they don't respect that, well, that is something very good to know about them, isn't it?

***

Veronica writes:

Oh yeah, NO... who knew? When I started saying NO first and then giving myself time to check in about how I felt, my life changed. What else is there to add?

Preferences/Judgments

Judgment is not the same as preference. Judgment is the belief that you have to have a position *against* something in order to have a position *preferring* something. So, all of a sudden the choice between chocolate and vanilla must become, "Chocolate is a good flavor and vanilla is a bad flavor, so I am going with chocolate because that's the good flavor," instead of just saying, "I have a preference for chocolate."

You're an immortal, infinite soul that chooses to have every experience you can manage. If you set out a lot of judgments and you start saying that vanilla's wrong, then when it comes around time to experience vanilla you have to deal with the baggage of already assigning it as "wrong." It's always nice to not put extra baggage on things that you'll probably get around to wanting to experience someday. It's also quite helpful to limit the amount of baggage (static) about anything you are experiencing.

Most of the time, we see that you had to make one thing wrong—sometimes VERY wrong—in order to set a preference because you weren't feeling strong enough to just say "No" is a complete sentence.

When you are new to boundaries and preferences you will sometimes believe that you have to get really worked up in order to use

them. Actually, when you discover "What is true now?," you can
set boundaries and state preferences from a very calm place.

Keep in mind that there is a damned good reason for having a
preference, which is: You're a soul experiencing the physical form
in a free-will zone. So, if you don't have some preferences, what
the heck is the point of being here in the first place? Not very
much that we can see. Having preferences is the one of the main
events!

Someone once said to us, "Well, if we are infinite and immortal,
aren't we going to do everything?" And we said yes, but you do
them in an order. There's an order to it. In a linear sense, there's an
order to it. Where today you decided to eat chocolate, tomorrow
you're going to decide to eat vanilla. So, even if you're immortal
and infinite, you're still deciding right now to be here instead of
being someplace else. Preference. Choice. Free will. You don't need
to have something be wrong in order to have something else be
what you want to do.

Coming from judgment is low-vibrational. It takes a lot of energy
to stay invested in a judgment. It can be difficult to change your
mind because you are so invested energetically in the judgment.
Sometimes your identity can even be wrapped up in a judgment,
which makes it that much harder to change. Judgments don't serve
you, on so many levels.

***

Veronica writes:

*Another tool to help you realize that you get to choose. This one helps
me clarifies when I am actually choosing and when I am running an
unconscious habit, which shows up as a judgment. I like vanilla and
chocolate ice cream so this example is perfect for me. It really is expressing a preference in the moment rather than deciding on a right/wrong.*

***

*This tool has whittled down my list of people, situations, and things that
I have judgments around and helps me realize how many judgments*

came through societal conditioning. Preferences allow for choice through fascination and true passion of my life's purpose. It brings me closer to the relaxed feeling of contentment and fulfillment.

—*Deb*

Shovel or ladder

The choice for consciousness is challenging, but habitual response is a pit of pain.

You get a shovel or a ladder; it's your choice to dig yourself in deeper or to climb up the ladder and out of the pit. The shovel is repeating habit; it's you not being willing to say, "What the hell is going on here inside me? Not with him, not with her, not with the boss, not with the kids, not with the bank, not with the credit card statement but within me?"

"Am I going to dig myself in deeper out of fear, guilt, lack, victimhood, or am I going to put my hand on the ladder and say something has to change? And am I going to keep climbing the ladder even when my pit partners look at me and say, 'What are you doing? Where are you going? Who do you think you are? You're getting too big for your britches!'" and all those other lines that they might give you. The ladder isn't just a hop. You're so far down in these pits of habitual response that you need one of those tall ladders, but the beauty is your ladder is tall enough.

You figure it out by putting one foot in front of the other and continuing to make the choices that say, "Habit is not who I am." Because when habit gets to tell you who you are, the scenery doesn't change. Do you want a shovel or a ladder? We will not give you shovels. But we have loads of ladders of all different sizes, shapes, and lengths and we even know how to make them taller. So if you get dug down in there, don't think you're ever lost. You're not ever lost in the pit of habit. You simply have to keep making the choice.

We're standing there cheering you on. Just lift your foot. We know it's challenging to break habits, but it will get easier. If you want your life to change, you need to choose and choose again to climb the ladder of consciousness.

***

Veronica writes:

When Eloheim first came up with this one, I was blown away. It is classic Eloheim, funny and practical. I picture them standing at the top of the hole saying, "We have ladders for you!" There is something so comforting about the image of them standing in the light looking at us down in the dark just waiting for us to reach up for the ladder they are lowering.

***

When dealing with a coworker who flips into hysteria/doom and gloom thinking when confronted with a problem, I find it helpful to use the Shovel (are you really sure you want to dig that great big huge hole for yourself?) / Ladder (don't you think we might actually get a better overview of this problem from up here?) approach. I used to call this the "Take the noose off your neck and get down from that chair" maneuver. But I like shovel/ladder now because it actually offers an alternative way of thinking about the situation rather than just a plea for different behavior.

—Rene

This emotion is a choice

One of the best ways to practice this tool is when you're watching TV or a movie—one of those things that are very, very carefully designed to elicit a certain emotion in you. Be very aware of the fact that you're being manipulated. Recognize that the emotion you're having is an emotion that has many layers to it. And one layer is manipulated creation and another layer is habit and another layer is authentic empathy with the person or situation.

Let yourself have the emotion, but know why you're having it. And if all of a sudden, you feel sad or upset and you don't know why you're feeling that way, then ask yourself, "Is there any good reason to be having this emotion? And if there isn't, then what can I ascertain about the state I'm in? This emotion has no basis, in the reality of this moment."

Your society places a lot of credence in "dealing with your emotions," without any real investigation of what you're feeling or why, or that you have any choice in the matter. This is where our example of the math problem comes in. What if we say: "What's 9,897,209.5 times 8,239,203?" You wouldn't take the first number that comes to mind as the right answer. Yet you'll take the first emotion that comes in as an indisputably correct position. If you find yourself in an emotion that doesn't seem actually relevant to the moment, be kind to yourself about it. Just remind yourself, "Oh yeah, that's right, the first emotion that trips along isn't necessarily the one I want to run with."

***

Veronica writes:

OH, BOY! Yep, this one is a good one. The freedom! The freedom of saying, "I get to choose." As a very sensitive person, I never even thought it was possible not to be swept away by other's emotions, feelings, or attitudes. This tool really helps me be conscious of how those things are affecting me.

***

Becoming skilled at neutral observation helps me to recognize when I am experiencing an emotion that doesn't feel good in my body. Where before, I might feel anger and try to make a story about that feeling so I could understand it, now I have some space to look at the feeling and simply label it: anger rising into tight shoulders. No story needed. Breathe. Thank the body for a signal. Choose to admit the feeling without judgment. Be curious together. Choose to love myself and the other by being vulnerable in the fact of the emotion, and choose gratitude for the closeness that arises instead of the anger-story's isolation.

—Margy Henderson

This is happening for me

Victims say, "Why is this happening to me?"

Creators say, "Why is this happening for me?"

Everything that is happening is happening for your growth.

Your world and everything in it—from these walls, to the lamp, to the camera, to our voice—is here for you and your play, for your journey as a soul experiencing a physical form. So when you shift into, "This is happening for me," you get to see how important it all is. It's all happening for you to grow. The fact that this planet is here spinning right now is for you. It's for you.

It was created for you to have this experience, the experience of having a car run into you, the experience of meeting a new lover, the experience of feeling like a victim—all of your experiences are happening for you. As you raise your consciousness level you have the opportunity to start letting all these things that are happening for you collaborate with your intention. When you feel like a victim and it's happening to you, you're sort of in a blender, spinning around. When it's happening for you, you're running the blender.

APPLYING THIS TOOL TO PAIN:

When you get an ache or a pain the temptation is so strong to say, "Oh, I wish I didn't have that pain," or "Oh, I feel old," or "I'm broken." Let's change that habit into "What is this teaching me?" "Why is this happening for me?" Because if you think about it and you want it to go away, you're not accepting that it's happening, and if you're not accepting it's happening, it can't change. It has to keep happening to keep asking you the same question. A pain in your body is asking you a question or raising a red flag, and if you just make it go away or ignore it, you are losing out on the chance of knowing what it's trying to tell you.

***

Veronica writes:

I use this one like a mantra. Sometimes I just say it over and over again to remind myself that I am a creator. It is very powerful when used that way.

***

As a family member was dying 500 miles away, knowing I was closest both emotionally and physically, I was called on and helped as best I was able to do. I started by offering her options for quality-of-life with significant self-care. After extended struggles with red tape and appropriate California documentation, I found a loving place for her to live... or die. The whole time I visited her, and also maintained her residence and her financial affairs, I kept choosing to progress with my own journey.
While this was a most strenuous time with my body still in recovery, the emotional climax was both easeful and graceful. I assured myself often that this is happening for me.
—Heidi Schunke

***

This is happening for me reminds me I am the creator of my experiences and keeps me personally empowered all the time.
—Randy Sue Collins

***

I love this tool! It inspires me to be in a childlike place—full of wonder and open—I always know I'll get an answer if I look. Just the other day, I had an appointment with an acupuncturist who turned out to be a psychiatrist as well. I wasn't so amenable to his 3-minute-consultation and extremely painful treatment. When I expressed my preferences and set some boundaries he mocked me and told me all the reasons I needed to come back, referencing my childhood and mother (whom he had never met) for added punch. I could have gone into confusion or victim mode and dwelled on his perception of me, but when I asked why this was happening for me, I got it—the situation was showing me that I really knew myself and I could trust myself to take care of myself, however that looked. This realization was transforming. Whether he was a sort of Ericksonian genius or not (I sort of doubt it...), I really got how that situation was a gift! It is so empowering to see experiences from this perspective.

—Anna R., Mexico

Velcro

Velcro has two different sides, a loop side and a hook side, and it only works if you have both sides. We want you to not have Velcro for the judgments of others. Don't have Velcro on your side. Just don't have it.

You have silver hair. If we said to you: "Wow, you have ugly black hair." Your response would be, "I don't have black hair." You have no Velcro for that judgment.

If, however, we said, "Wow, you have ugly silver hair," it might be more challenging to not have Velcro for our judgment. But, it's still your choice. Use your free will to decide.

Another important place to look for Velcro is in your judgments about yourself. When you stop having inner Velcro for your judgment about yourself, it makes it much easier to not have Velcro for the judgments of others.

This tool is very important. Ask yourself, "Do I have Velcro—even empathically—do I have Velcro for it?" And you do. But you don't need to. Now that you're alerted to that, you can re-evaluate whether or not you want to have Velcro on any subject.

***

Veronica writes:

As a sensitive, psychic, empathic, channel, etc., I was a walking Velcro strip. Not only in the ways that Eloheim describes here, but with the feelings of others. I really got this tool and have used it countless times. When I realize I am picking up on others' energy I can say, "Don't have Velcro for that." And then shift to What is true now? to check in with what I am actually experiencing.

***

Velcro is a nifty tool. I use it to bring awareness of issues that need my immediate attention. It's fun to see where issues that once had Velcro no longer do.

—Murster

What am I afraid of?

What is this going to cost me if I open up emotionally here, if I am vulnerable?

What do I think is going to happen? What's the big, scary fear? What's the big, scary outcome that I'm avoiding? Looking at your fear helps reveal the issue that needs to be dealt with.

When you find yourself triggered or disturbed or upset, ask, "What am I afraid of?" as an empowering question. It's not a gateway into feeling more fear, it's an inquiry into knowing what your fears are.

Every time you can do that, you're interrupting that habitual flow toward the fear-based paradigm and you're wonderfully reinserting the consciousness-based paradigm. The nice thing is there is no middle ground. It's either fear-based paradigm or consciousness-based paradigm. So, when you're not responding with fear, you're responding with consciousness, so you're investing in that shift of perspective every single time.

***

Veronica writes:

What am I afraid of? Just about everything, or so it seemed! I was a very fearful child and full of fear as an adult. This tool really helped me put a face on that fear rather than let it run me around. This is a great tool to combine with What is true now, Neutral observation, and What's in your lap.

***

The tool What am I afraid of brings me out of the fear-based operating system and into the consciousness-based operating system. It brings me into neutral observation, into the now, my body relaxes and stops the emotion. I don't always have the answer, but sometimes I am shown layers of old habitual thinking usually anchored in victim energy.

—Marilyn

What is true now?

Asking yourself "What is true now?" is a way of staying connected to the moment and your soul's insight about the moment.

It's fairly easy to remember to say "What is true now," but it's also very easy to be habitual about the answer you allow yourself to experience. What is true now is not answered by the mind. What is true now is answered by an "aha" from the soul, so by asking yourself what is true now constantly, you're creating a very strong connection between you and your soul, which is a fine thing to do if you're interested in transforming your life. The truth of you must be experienced consciously.

If what is true now is answered by a sentence of, say, more than say 10 words, it's your mind. An "aha" from the soul is going to be shorter than that. It doesn't need to be lengthy because it's not processed by the mind. It's an energetic truth expressed briefly in order to really sink in. If what is true now starts to have a lengthy explanation, suspect that the mind is encroaching on the soul's turf and ask the mind to shut up.

When used with consistency and consciousness, what is true now can be used to uncover unconscious coping mechanisms and lies that you tell yourself.

Veronica writes:

Another tool to keep very close to you. I use this one a lot to help sort out when I am acting from my current preferences and when I am acting habitually or out of patterns from the past.

***

I like "What is true now." I find the greatest challenge is being aware when the chatter-y monkey-mind starts with its unsuspectingly clever maneuvering to make me feel uncomfortable or irritated or going around and around on the same conversation. Old news, stuff that is past its expiry date, as they say. When I realize it, I immediately go to "What is true now." What is usually "true now" is that I was enjoying whatever I was doing before the sneaky bits got into my conscious thoughts. It seems never-ending.

—*Rosie*

What's in your lap?

When you are tempted to get into somebody else's business or find yourself judging people and/or events, ask yourself "What's in my lap? What is going on in me? How does this reflect something in me?" You can't tell anybody else what they need to see or what they are seeing; you need to deal with what's in your lap.

Are you in this moment? What static are you aware of? Where are you lying to yourself? What are you afraid of?

Need we go on? There is PLENTY for you to focus on right there in your lap.

***

Veronica writes:

I love this, "Need we go on?" Eloheim specifically told me to put that in there.

***

I use this tool a lot when I'm triggered by my birth family. We have a lot of issues around lack that we've been working out with each other from the time we were children. So now, when one of my siblings calls to complain about not having enough money, I look at what it brings up in me, what's in my lap, and it helps me to not go into "savior" mode. When I am conscious about this, it amazes me how much the conversation can change.

—Claire

Where am I lying to myself?

What things do you have a hard time admitting to yourself? What are the things you don't want anyone else to know? What are the things you have kept hidden?

In order to realize your authentic expression, you can't be lying to yourself. "Where are the holdout places where I'm telling myself stories about who I am?" They're typically going to be around one of these areas: sex, money, relationships, job, health, and housing.

"Where am I lying to myself about my marriage?" The word lying is such a triggering word but we are using it on purpose, because in essence you're lying to yourself if you know your marriage isn't working for you and you don't say that to yourself. Don't fall into the belief that you have to act on this awareness, simply allow yourself to be conscious of what your truth is. This one step is powerfully transformative.

What is the truth that you haven't told yourself or you've hidden from other people? What's the thing you're embarrassed people will know about you? What is the thing you're trying not to think about all the time? "What is true now?" reveals the things that *can serve you*, "Where am I lying to myself?" reveals the things that you wish *you could ignore*. Where you lie to yourself generates static in your life.

***

Veronica writes:

*At first, I thought this was going to be the same as What is true now?,
but it is quite different. What is true now? helps me come back to the
moment. Where am I lying to myself? helps me see why I don't want
to be in the moment in the first place. Make sure to be nice to yourself
when you discover where you are lying to yourself. It is easy to slip into
judgment.*

Who answers the door? The current version of you

A PRACTICAL EXAMPLE:

The ex-boyfriend is banging on the front door, you go to answer it but you don't want to talk to him—ask yourself, "Who answers the door?"

Does the four-year-old who's looking for her daddy's approval answer the door? Does the 20-year-old who just wants a boyfriend because she doesn't want to be alone answer the door? Does the 40-year-old who doesn't want to be divorced answer the door? Or does the you of the now that knows that guy shouldn't be in your life answer the door? Who answers the door? You decide that.

This tool is empowering because you say, "OK, I'm not bringing the 4-, 20-, or 40-year-old into this. The current version of me knows that I no longer want this guy in my life. The current version of me can say, 'No'." The four-year-old probably wouldn't be able to say no because the 4-year-old's still looking for daddy to make it right, and the 20-year-old still feels like she did something wrong, so she's going to have a hard time saying no, the 40-year-old's feeling like he might be her last chance at love, so she's not turning him away.

But in the moment where you bring your high-vibrational self together and you look at that person and you say, "In this moment, with who I am right now, this situation is not OK, and you need to leave. Off you go. The door's getting locked behind you." And then you turn the ringer off on the phone and you just sit with the fact that you actually made a decision based on who you are today. That's where you give yourself the gift of being who you are today and living your life from who you are today, rather than allowing all baggage from the past or projecting into the future.

USING THIS TOOL WITH FAMILY MEMBERS:

A lot of times, when you're working with biological relatives, the stuff that you're learning about is the stuff from when you were five. However, now you're 40 and you're still doing your five-year-old shit, often from a five-year-old's perspective. Work on the issue when you're 40 as a forty-year-old, rather than, "I'm 40 but I'm acting like I'm five, which I've been doing for 35 years with my mom." This gives you a better chance of success, or a different chance of success, of actually learning and growing and becoming more of who you are.

Yes, you can say, "There's something for me to learn here, but my God, me as a 40-year-old trying to act like an eight-year-old with my mom who is now 70, is not working." It's not working and you have the right to say, "I want to learn this some other way."

This is loving yourself, giving yourself permission to set boundaries across your life. Set the boundaries you need to set in order to give yourself the best chance at learning what it is you desire to learn.

***

Veronica writes:

I remember so clearly the first time Eloheim talked about this tool. I was channeling in a living room facing the front door, so it was very visceral imagining the ex-boyfriend on the other side. I have used this tool time and time again in almost every sort of situation. Definitely one of my favorites.

***

I have used this tool, especially with my birth family members, where it was easy to slip into being a 10-year-old again. I no longer do that. I now respond and create from the person I am in the moment.

—Randy Sue Collins

You can't have change without change

"I don't like my job!"

"Why don't you look for a new one?"

"Oh, I couldn't do that!"

This pattern is so common. Your desire for transformation and your fear of change pull you in different directions. The result is suffering and the tendency to live from habit.

To experience change, you have to know what to do with fear and evolve your relationship to the survival instinct. This is a core requirement on the path of ascension.

You cannot experience transformation unless something transforms. You cannot alter your paradigm unless there is an alteration of your perspective.

***

Veronica writes:

Short, sweet, and to the point. It's amazing how many times people have come to Eloheim for advice and it has sounded like the example above. Do you want change? Then something has to be allowed to change within you!

***

This is one of my favorite tools. It allows me to open the door and dare to dream—BIG! It takes the stale and stagnant out of life for me.

—Randy Sue Collins

***

Here is a physical lesson to make this tool clear. Our yard was surrounded with a thick group of trees creating a lush and contained, secure-feeling environment. One crashed down, with the fence, too. We were first devastated as the loss of our beautiful 20-foot-high natural wall. Then we looked farther and realized we could see many more stars, like we had long ago before they grew so tall and wide. Also, we could see a few miles to the mountains and the sunrise. All hidden before. Now changed. Then we lost another huge tree and a second tree's healthy limb, which left a very wide swath of nothing, no greenery, no strength, no buffer from the world. The old guard was gone. And we can see far now, our view expanded to the near hill. We set up new boundaries to this new world, and built a fence just high enough, but not so high as to block out the other parts of the world that we are just newly able to see.

—Rosie

You to you (compare)

Stop and pat yourself on the back every once in a while, won't you? Your inner truth is externalized through your life, and a lot of times it's the crappy bits that you notice. But we want you to start paying attention to the bits that reflect an internal journey that's actually moving toward bliss, that's actually on a transformational path. Because that's the truth of it. The truth of it is that you're on a transformational path and things are changing and it's easy to get lost in the changes if they're challenging. But the truth is, comparing you to you, you are transforming. And you need to be patting yourself on the back, giving yourself credit, and mentioning to your friends the things that are transforming in you in order to give them the kind of publicity within you that the shitty bits get. Publicize your transformation. Or at least notice it, at a minimum.

You are constantly in a pattern of transformation. If you don't do compare you to you, you're likely to feel like you are in one never-ending problem. When you compare you to you, you stop for a moment to realize, "Well, this is a different thing I'm dealing with now. That other issue shifted, so maybe I can try those tools with this new trigger."

Veronica writes:

This tool has such a loving feeling to it. You are making progress. You are transforming. You are changing. It is happening. Stop and allow yourself to see it. Love yourself for the progress you have made. Be fascinated by the journey yet to come.

***

I'm so focused on moving forward all the time, I sometimes forget to do this. But when I remember this tool, I love myself for who I am—again.

—*Randy Sue Collins*

***

Compare you to you allows me to step out of an old situation and instantly reevaluate it with a fresh outlook.

—*Mike*

***

Comparing me to me in stressful situations has been both fascinating and encouraging. There is always a gem of progress to be seen and felt that keeps my heart light and gives me courage to keep on keeping on.

—*Deb*

***

I find this tool extremely helpful in measuring my progress over time. How would a similar issue have affected me in the past? "Compare you to you" is a perfect measuring stick for gauging personal growth.

—*Murster*

***

Compare U2U is such an affirming tool. It is so great to feel the progress I'm making. It is so sweet and so fair to leave everyone else out of the picture and just relish how far I've come. Nothing inspires like success, right?

—*Anna R., Mexico*

Terms

2012

The year 2012 is a shifting point on your calendar, a place of attention in order to help you focus. This is not a deadline, but a focal point to help facilitate your desire for consciousness and your desire for transformation. It is not a fixed point in time. The "place" of 2012 is a potential for dramatic transformation. That "place" is meeting you where you are; from there, you create the transformation that you desire both as a human and as a soul.

3D

Shorthand term for expressing the soul incarnate in the physical form, experiencing duality, density, and running the fear-based operating system. 3D is the status quo human condition prior to the shift to Homo spiritus.

4 billion

There are at least 4 billion people on the planet who won't agree with you, won't like you, or will never meet you. This number is likely underestimated. When we say, "Oh, you have found one of the 4 billion," it is not to dismiss or diminish their views, but to comfort you that this is a common phenomenon and put it into a perspective that hopefully helps you manage any triggers that come up. The energetics of this idea are similar to saying, "There are other fish in the sea."

5D

Shorthand term for expressing the soul experiencing the human form with a consciousness-based operating system. 5D is the experience of Homo spiritus, where the body is lived from an ensouled perspective.

Abundance

Abundance and "your abundant nature" are terms to describe the energetics reflecting the dynamic scope of possibility offered at this time, a concept meant to reflect the infinite possibilities (of all types) that exist in your physical world.

Our favorite way to illustrate the concept of true abundance is to have people look at how much nature surrounds them, for example: grass, trees, air, sky, and clouds. When one finds oneself lacking abundance, it is important to remember that abundance always exists in nature, and that is the place to start. You can also look at people smiling, hair on people's heads, or how many people have shoes. The point is to find a way to look into the world and see that there is much abundance.

The term abundance has also been corrupted to mean great sums of money or hoarding. Abundance, as an expanded definition, requires that one breaks the cycle or releases the belief that abundance only reflects how much money one has or how many houses one owns, to instead reflect any place where there is plenty or plentifulness. One simply needs to shift one's perspective about what plenty or abundance is.

Aha

A moment of clarity and insight that comes from accessing the soul's perspective; contrast this with the repetitive hamster-wheel-mind habit of thinking.

Ahas are commonly experienced while in the shower or doing other tasks that don't require full attention. The path of ascension and the choice for consciousness facilitate experiencing a steady stream of ahas.

Akashic Record

The galactic Internet.

A term that reflects the totality of: all of the lifetimes of those who have experienced Earth, all of the time that one has spent between lifetimes, all of the time spent in other incarnational opportunities, and all the time spent as a soul doing whatever the soul wanted to do. Think of a giant library where you each have your own section or file containing everything that has ever been recorded regarding what you've done, how you've lived, and what you've encountered. This isn't kept in anything that would resemble a library but it is helpful to think of it in this way conceptually.

Your Akashic Record is a reservoir of information that makes up the body of your soul. The energy that reflects that reservoir of information is what would be correlated to the physicality of the soul, if the soul had physicality.

When you are not in body and encounter another soul, your section of the Akashic Records is the information presented to the other soul. Your Akashic Record is the information that your soul presents to other souls at first glance.

Alternate expressions

Your "past and future" lives. Since time is not linear, these so-called "past and future" lives are all happening simultaneously; therefore your "other" lives can be referred to as alternate expressions of you.

Amnesia

The term we use to describe the "clean slate" of forgetfulness that a human experiences to facilitate living in physical form. It is a necessary state of being to incarnate into the physical body. Amnesia allows you to focus on the present moment in the present lifetime, without distractions from other lifetimes.

If you did not have amnesia about previous Earth experiences and incarnations it would be virtually impossible to stay in the moment because you'd be too busy wanting to go finish, redo, or undo things that have happened in alternate expressions.

Appreciation brings you into the moment

The high-vibrational space of love, appreciation, and fascination stops the thinking and clears the way for your soul's insight to drop in.

By appreciating yourself, you bring yourself into the space where you love yourself well. Appreciation is a very high-vibrational state. It's quite magnetic; it attracts other high-vibrational states.

Ascension

Ascension is a gradual, albeit drastic, transformation from a fear-based operating system into a consciousness-based operating system. Ascension requires evolution in the physical form and a radical shift in the way you respond to the biological messages the body offers.

Ascension is the term assigned to the energetic of the evolutionary leap into Homo spiritus. The Homo spiritus energetic allows for a life to be lived from the soul's perspective, and for a transformed way of interacting with physical matter.

Ascension does not mean you're leaving the body or the planet. Ascension means you're experiencing being in-body on Earth in a brand-new way that is a higher-vibrational, conscious way of living from your soul's perspective in which a spiritual partnership is formed between the soul, physical form, and personality self.

Audience or opinion

Sometimes, people just want an audience for their ramblings/complaining and aren't actually looking for connection. Be cautious about matching energy and lowering your vibration in these situations.

Aura

A way of describing the energy field that surrounds objects, people, animals, and even places. Another way of describing the emanation of individuality; the emanation of the truth of you.

A person's aura is most easily perceivable 4–8 feet from the body; however, auras extend out infinitely.

Baggage

The past, future, cultural pressures, DNA pressures, habits, triggers, and other static that get in the way of you experiencing the moment.

Being a question mark

Each of you has a question that you have incarnated to explore. The broad way of stating this question is, "Who am I?"

You're a question. Your soul asks a question and the exploration of the question—not the answer, but the exploration of the question—is you and your purpose of being in the body at this time.

"What is the question I am answering by the current way I am living? What is the question I'm exploring by my expression?" consciously knowing you are in a questioning state is very important. Nothing is actually certain. When you make peace with certainty being a fallacy, you then say, "Well, what am I experiencing instead?"

You're in the question of you as you anticipate clarity coming in, not to answer the question but to give you the next step on the road of exploring the question that you are living. Clarity is not a stopping point. It is not a substitute for what you hoped certainty would be. It is simply an "aha" on the road of exploring the question of you that your soul is asking.

The question "Who am I?" does not go away simply because you have an aha about it in this moment. The question continues to exist. The questioning state is a permanent condition of your soul's nature.

"Who am I?" "Aha" and, "Who am I?" That's the path of consciousness. "Why am I here? Why am I doing this? Why, why, why, why?" The why doesn't need an answer. It is not about an outcome. Exploration of the why is a way to access the ever-unfolding truth of you. Your state of being is: "I am in why."

Bliss

The state of living in a spiritual partnership with your soul as a high-vibrational, conscious being. The state resulting from having tools for conscious living, being in neutral observation, and knowing that an experience previously judged as wrong (or right) is actually an opportunity for learning and growth. Living in a state of bliss is the result of living in the consciousness-based operating system as Homo spiritus.

Boundaries

Using your ability as a creator while living in a free-will zone to choose what you are interested in experiencing; directing the incarnation.

Boundaries with consequences

In order to leave fear, victimhood, and low-vibrational states behind, you set boundaries in the moment—boundaries with consequences. Boundaries without consequences are just hot air coming out of your mouth. For example, you might say, "You can't speak to me that way," and then the person speaks to you that way. If you don't then act (enact the consequences), all you're doing is blowing hot air. So, boundaries should have consequences attached for the person you're setting the boundary with: "This is what's acceptable in my life and if that doesn't work for you, then you're not in my life."

Is it hard to say to someone, "I'm setting a boundary with you and there are consequences attached"? Of course it is. Is it hard to continue the relationship without boundaries and feel like a victim all the time? We think that's harder.

Brain

Your brain is the biological functioning unit for thinking and it runs the body's processes. The brain also allows you to experience insight.

Bunnies and rainbows

You don't always have to put a smiley face on everything in order to be liked, loved, appreciated, understood, companioned. The way we like to say this is: It doesn't all have to be bunnies and rainbows.

EXAMPLES OF HOW THIS TERM IS USED:

You have to know what the truth of heart chakra energy is, and it's not bunnies and rainbows. It's not just love, love, love. It's loving yourself first.

***

The high-vibrational aspect of this situation isn't necessarily bunnies and rainbows. It's not, "I only want the bunnies and rainbows kind of thing out of that alternate expression." It's, "I want what's going to make me higher-vibrational, more conscious, in the now." So if you find yourself unable to love aspects of yourself, well, welcome to the shadowland. Welcome to an aspect of knowing what you need to work with. Why don't you love it? How can you say, "I love you" to that aspect of you? We are not going to fall for any, "I love you because you are bright and shiny and bunnies and rainbows." If you don't love something about yourself it is more conscious to say, "I don't love me" than it is to say, "Well I'm going to love me" or "I have to say I love me."

***

It's not as much that you have to say "I need to love it" or "I need it to have light" or any of those things. It's not, "OK, yes, my knee hurts; let's get the bunnies and rainbows out." It's, "Yes, my knee hurts and it's teaching me." So, say yes to what it is and then work with it, but continue to remind yourself of that "yes" to what it is.

***

The moment isn't a bunnies-and-rainbows spot, and a lot of times in some of the literature that's out there they say, "Oh, just be in the moment and all will be well." Well, that's crap. Be in the moment and you will start to experience the intensity that's available to you as a Homo spiritus individual. It is intense and it does ask a lot of you, but that's why you have lots and lots of tools to support your journey. The moment isn't necessarily going to be silence. It's not meditation. It's an opening to an enormous amount of insight, an enormous amount of information, and an enormous amount of opportunity to live differently in the *next* moment, to create differently for the *next* moment, to move differently into the *next* moment.

***

"Perfect" doesn't mean "feels good." Perfect is not bunnies and rainbows. Perfect is not easy. What is perfect? Precisely what is needed to give you the handhold on the climbing wall of ascension that you need right now.

***

Healing is an interesting word. By healing we don't necessarily mean: "Is it happy, happy, joy, joy, bunnies and rainbows?" No. By healing we mean: "Do I grow? Do I transform? Do I like myself more? Do I feel like I'm a better person? Am I becoming more of the truth of me?"

But and because

We use "but and because" as a red flag to alert you that you may be slipping into victim mentality. If you find yourself using those words, you may be leaving the realm of "I created it" and entering into the position of "it was done to me." Listen to conversation around you and begin to notice how frequently you hear "because this" and "but that."

At times, you may feel like you need to include a "but" or a "because" to feel like you have conveyed your entire story. That may be the case. We are not saying that you should remove them from your language completely. We are suggesting that you become conscious of how you use "but" and "because." We believe it will help uncover places where you are habituating to victimhood.

An example from a conversation about income streams:

You said, "Yeah, I have 35 different ways money comes to me, *but* I still can't pay my bills." Instead say, "I have 35 ways money comes to me. Period."

"But and because" take away your high-vibrational state, they lower your energetic, make it more difficult to reach insight from your soul, and cause you to slip back into thinking, thinking, thinking. Remember, if thinking could have solved it, it would've solved it long ago, because you sure have thought about it enough. We aren't looking to think more, we are seeking insight.

AN EXAMPLE FROM A CONVERSATION ABOUT TRYING NEW THINGS:

You are tempted to say: "Oh, but I couldn't; oh, but I don't; oh, but that's silly; oh, but, oh, but." Right? It does not serve you to "but-and-because" away a fascination. A fascination is present for a reason. The exploration of the fascination is the gift, the gift you give yourself. What exactly do you think your soul's perspective is going to feel like? Souls are very curious. They want to learn and grow and do new things. Is it surprising that the soul's perspective comes in as fascination and curiosity?

Certainty

When you are operating from the fear-based operating system, change feels extremely risky. The survival instinct is constantly pressuring you to stay the same, because "the same" has kept you alive. Any changes to "the same" require certainty about the outcome in order to quiet the fears the survival instinct produces. As certainty is a fallacy—you can't be truly certain of anything in the diverse, vast world you find yourself in—you find yourself in a no-win situation: Change requires certainty, certainty is unattainable, and paralysis (fear) is the result.

Evolving your relationship to the survival instinct and certainty is a major aspect of the ascension process.

Chakra

Energy centers in the body. Traditionally, there are seven major chakras: Root (1st), Sexuality (2nd), Power (3rd), Heart (4th), Throat (5th), Third eye (6th), and Crown (7th). We use the idea of chakras as a handy reference tool. It's a shortcut that allows us to talk about different aspects of your body and energetic system without having to go into a long explanation each time. It is not required that you believe in chakras to follow the conversation.

Change

The recognition of an altered condition in the incarnation, which, if processed habitually, often triggers fear. When processed consciously, change becomes the mechanism for growth.

Channel

An incarnated soul experiencing the human form that allows non-physical guides to communicate through him or her in order to present helpful information in a palatable form. If out-of-body or non-corporal guides showed up as a burning bush, beam of light, or in a light body of some fashion, they would be far more likely to create fear than comfort. Channeling and channels allow a more human-to-human type of transmission of information, commonly less triggering than other types of transmissions.

Channeled message

Information that comes through a channel from guides that are not in physical form, but have perspective on the physical journey or the human experiment.

Checking things off your list

You incarnated into this lifetime with what we call a "list" of things that you hoped to do. The list includes experiences you wanted to have, things that you were interested in doing, unfinished business, experiences that you wanted to try again, or plans you made with other souls. You and your soul started this list before you ever incarnated into the physical form and it has carried over throughout all the incarnations you have experienced here on Earth.

What tends to happen is that as things on your list "come up," you check off the things that are less triggering, less challenging, and less difficult first. The items that are more difficult are often passed over to be dealt with another time. As you get closer and closer to the last few items on your list, they can feel very difficult. They feel more difficult because every time you said, "Oh no! I'm not ready to do that item right now, I'm going to do something else!" the item acquired a charge of impossibility. If you have re-queued the same issue many times, the charge of impossibility can feel quite large.

A lot of you have several things that have been on your list over many lifetimes of which you are very energetically frightened. Every time they've come up, you haven't been able to handle them. Now that you're at a higher-vibrational level than you've ever been with more awareness and tools, these things don't need to be anywhere near as scary as they used to be. In fact, you are more prepared to handle them than you have ever been before. In essence, you were clever by procrastinating! How often do you get to hear that?

The tricky part is that although you are now energetically prepared to experience these last few things on your list, the habit of fright is so deep that it can get in the way of looking at it from today's perspective and being able to say, "What's really going on here?" It's easy to lose sight of the fact that you have more tools and ability to handle them than ever before, but once you wade into them, they usually are much easier to deal with than you had imagined. It's just about being courageous enough to experience them after so many lifetimes of being so fearful.

Choose your reactions to your creations

"I am 100 percent responsible for my reactions to my creations." That's one of the most conscious things you can say. We strongly recommend that you write that down and stick it on your bathroom mirror.

"I am a creator; I created it all. It's all here *for* me, and I choose how I react to my creations as well." When something occurs, don't look for it to be different. Don't say, "I wish it were some other way." Say, "What is here right now is here on purpose. It's here because it needs to be here to facilitate my growth." Then, take it further; take your acknowledgment of the truth of you as a creator to the point where you can also say, "I am choosing the reaction I have to every single experience in my life. All of it."

It is your responsibility to set boundaries, state preferences, tell the truth about your creations, and to make sure that your creations bring out the authenticity of you, which you can then share. That's the gift of creating and choosing your reactions to your creations; it lets you share the truth of you. Consistently emanate the truth of you regardless of the circumstances you find yourself in by choosing your reactions based on your high-vibrational, conscious experiences of yourself.

Compassion

The traditional use of this word is very low-vibrational, as it tends toward victimization. Every experience is here to teach you something. Every experience is here as an opportunity for growth. When you feel compassion for someone, be very cautious that you are not casting them as a victim of their circumstances. You can say, "Wow, that seems like a tough way to learn, can I support you as you experience it?" But it is low-vibrational to say, "I feel sorry for you," or any other comment that implies the situation wasn't chosen.

This isn't a very romantic way to express what has been termed compassion, and may even feel harsh. However, you are either a victim or a creator. You can't be both. Exploring your creations (even if you have no conception of why you would have created them) is the path of consciousness and ascension.

Complex vs. complicated

Complex is fine. Complex is interesting. Complex is plenty of stuff going on and your brain likes it and your body likes it and your soul, of course, likes it.

Complicated is static. Complicated is low vibration. Complicated is unconscious. Complicated is, "Oh God, I have to make sure this person is happy," and "Oh God, I have to look after that person," and "Oh God…" this, that and the other thing. Complicated doesn't serve you.

Complex fascinates you. Complicated confuses you.

Complicated feels like there are no answers. Complex feels like "Oh, I get to put this puzzle together." Complicated feels like "All the puzzle pieces are the same color and someone's screaming at me while I'm trying to build it."

So, use "complicated" as a red flag. When it's complicated, look closely; it's an opportunity to become more conscious!

Conscious/Consciousness

Knowing why you do what you do. Choosing your reactions. Not being driven by habit. Experiencing the world as a creator rather than as a victim.

The world, as you experience it, has been programmed through habits, fears, and your biology. Through attention (consciousness), you can live the bigger picture that includes your personality's paradigm shifting and the embracing of your soul's perspective, as well.

Consciousness-based operating system (CBOS)

The consciousness-based operating system is the 5D or Homo spiritus way of experiencing the world that allows for conscious interactions with experiences rather than fear-based, habitually driven interaction with experiences.

Core Emotion (CE)

Your core emotion is a theme present in every thought, action, feeling, dream, hope, experience, and desire. It is present in all moments of your life. Your core emotion is unique to you and unique to this lifetime. Discovering your core emotion often answers long-standing questions such as: "Why does this keep happening?" "Why do all my relationships follow the same pattern?" "Why can't I get past this blockage in my path?"

Most people experience their core emotion from an unconscious or unhealed perspective. Learning to work with your core emotion from a healed or conscious perspective is often described as "life-changing." Since the core emotion is present in all aspects of your life, bringing consciousness to the core emotion brings consciousness to all aspects of your life.

NOTE: The exploration of your core emotion is one of our specialties. We have a specific process for revealing your core emotion and helping you move from an unhealed to a healed relationship with it. Because of the intensely personal nature of this exploration and the time required to fully explore it, we only offer this process through private sessions. For more information, see the Contact section on page 127.

Courage
Awareness of the temptation to fear and other types of static, but making the choice to act from consciousness instead.

Courageous enough
Are you courageous enough to think about now instead of running habit with the hamster-wheel mind? Are you courageous enough to think about this moment rather than skipping over it?

Creating your reality
"Create your own reality" is one of those terms that's overused and under-understood. Creating your reality is often believed to be a way to *control* your reality. It is thought to be a path to certainty and safety. Creating your reality is actually an outcome of your vibrational self, your vibrational nature, your emanation of a higher-vibrational choice.

Creating your reality works very much like a fountain. The fountain shoots up the water and it sprays out all over the place. No one knows where every drop's going to land. Who would want to? It would be tedious in the extreme. The uncertainty creates the beauty.

Similarly, creating your reality isn't about the outcome (where the drops land), it is about the experience (the beauty of the water in the air.)

In our fountain example, the water represents the truth of you (your soul's perspective and your personality), the water pressure represents your free-will choices and the fountain mechanism represents your preferences and boundaries.

Creating your reality starts with setting boundaries in association with your preferences. You then align your free-will to choose conscious reactions to your experiences (which often has the result of clearing static), and then you and your soul emanate together.

You initiate your creation, you choose how you react to your creation, and you remain open to insight from your soul.

Creator, The

If you believe that this world is created, then there must be a Creator. Therefore, the Creator is the one who created all. It helps to recognize that the Creator is not conceivable in its entirety while experiencing duality because of the inherent limitations of the human mind and the infinite scope of the Creator. However, the Creator can be sensed through insight from your soul and through experiencing creation.

Creator/creatorship

As a creator, you are aware that you are in a free-will zone and that you have the ability to choose your reactions to your experiences. When creations seem to be in opposition to what you "want," creators recognize that there are levels of creation and that everything is happening *for* me, rather than falling into victimhood.

Cultural pressures

Cultural pressures include: family beliefs, societal norms, and customs. Often, cultural pressures present as, "It's what everyone else is doing" and are used to justify forgoing transformation.

Habits and DNA pressures combine with cultural pressures to make a potent combination for habitual response to triggers.

Density

Experiencing the free-will zone in a body. Souls do not have physical form in the same way humans do. Incarnating on Earth provides for the unique experience of density, duality, and free will.

Digging a ditch

If you've been digging a ditch for 50 years, it's pretty easy to dig it deeper. You already have the walls there, you already have the guidelines and the exact dimensions of the ditch, and you have a plan.

If you decide that you're going to dig a ditch in a new area, it requires a different kind of attention. You start off by marking the lines where you want the ditch to be. Then you need to figure out where you're going to take the dirt you remove, etc. The new project requires many new actions and perhaps even some new tools.

It's the same with changing habitual responses.

Instead of repeating old patterns, you're starting a whole new journey. That changeover requires some consistency. Sure, you can always go back to the "comfortable" old ditch, but we're pretty sure you have learned all you need to learn about that. Use spiritual discipline to focus on new, healthy patterns to get out of the old rut and open up your life.

DNA pressures

Your DNA is the blueprint for your body. You and your soul collaborated to create the unique incarnation you are experiencing.

We use the term "DNA pressures" to refer to the interaction habits and consciousness have with your physicality.

As an example: Tall people habitually put things on high shelves while shorter people will habitually put things on lower shelves. Both are examples of people acting based on DNA (and convenience).

DNA pressures combine with cultural pressures to make a potent combination for habitual response to triggers.

Don't bring your baggage to the moment

Your ability to neutrally observe your life without bringing anything to the moment. You don't gather things up from your past. You don't pull things in from the future. You don't allow your fears to be involved. You say, "What is this moment? I am experiencing only *this* moment."

Duality

The idea that there are only two options, typically experienced as either, "what I think is right and what I think is wrong," or "what they think is right and what they think is wrong." A very limited way to experience Earth and the human form. The fear-based operating system loves duality because it gives a false sense of certainty. (I am RIGHT). The consciousness-based operating system leaves duality behind as it explores the truth of, "Everything that happens, happens for me and is teaching me something."

Earth

The planet Earth is designated as a free-will zone and was developed to provide opportunities for incarnating souls to experience density and duality. Earth, at this time, is engaged in an ascension process and will reflect a changed environment for ascended beings to explore. What that changed environment will actually look like is unknown, and highly anticipated for that very reason.

Ease

Living in the human form while utilizing tools for conscious living.

Ease not easy

We never said it would be easy to ensoul your physical form and evolve your body. We never promised "easy," but we did commit to you that you could start living in ease.

Easy

Please, please, please, give up on the idea that "easy" means you're right or that "easy" means it's working. It's not about easy, meaning: no effort. It's about realization, moving through, handling and processing triggers, recognizing transformation, and allowing change in.

Allowing change in is almost always the final step because things start to shake out inside of you, you start to create in your external world, and then all of a sudden something has to change. Your relationship to your world starts to shift. And if you're not willing to take that final step and shift your relationship to your world, then you've done all that work and you're not actually enjoying it or experiencing it.

Part of what happens is you think, "Well, if it's not easy, it's not worth doing," or "It's not easy, so I don't want to," or "It's not easy, so I'm on the wrong path." It's not about easy. It's about looking at your world and saying, "I'm triggered and I want to transform it," or "this habit that I'm not happy with, I want to make it different," and then paying attention to it, which allows you to shift it and transform it into something else. That's the freedom here—paying attention to the thing that you become aware of and then sticking with it enough that you allow your life to shift around the change you've made.

What we really see happen is that you do a ton of internal work and then when it starts to appear in your world, asking you for something new, you resist the external change. There is the temptation to stay small even though the work has been done. The temptation to stay small has to be dealt with. That means taking the internal work and experiencing it externally, walking it, emanating it. Don't drop the ball on the last step. Because that's really where the rubber meets the road. Until then, it's all personal, but when you take it into the world, there can be that last little hurdle. At some point you have to stick your neck out in order to experience your changed life.

Eloheim

We, the Eloheim, are a collaboration of souls presenting with a singular voice, channeled through the body of Veronica Torres with her explicit approval, willingness, and allowance. It is our great privilege to offer our support to you at this very exciting time on Earth to facilitate the transformation of Homo sapiens to Homo spiritus; moving from the fear-based operating system to the consciousness-based operating system. It is a grand experiment that many beings in the universe are watching with great interest, awe, and fascination.

Emanating (the truth of you)

As you live consciously, you emanate consciousness into your world. Your job is just to contribute, your job is not to try to dictate or control where your contribution to high-vibrational living ends up. It's not your business where it goes or how it shows up in the world.

Energetics

The way that souls communicate through nonverbal knowing. Because your physical forms cannot yet communicate on the level that souls do, nonverbal knowing or "energetics" need to be translated into your language to facilitate understanding and communication.

Since it is always less accurate to use language than it is to communicate energetically, it is our hope and desire that your progress will eventually include the ability to communicate energetically without the need for language.

Energetic communication is happening all the time. Living consciously means that you are emanating a conscious energetic. It really does matter how you handle triggers and other upsets. Not just because it determines how you will experience the triggers, but it also determines how your emanation will go out to others. When we work with you, we are reading your energetics far more than we are listening to your words. Your energetics often show us visuals, which we can use to facilitate deeper understanding of the situations you are experiencing.

Ensoulment

The process by which soul energy is more deeply experienced by the personality incarnated in the physical form as the perspective is shifted from one of a survival instinct to a soul's perspective—from a fear-based operating system to a consciousness-based operating system.

Ensoulment, or living from the soul's perspective, is a collaboration between the personality self (you incarnate as a human) and your soul's wisdom. Don't misunderstand this to be that your soul "takes you over." This is not the case.

As an example, let's say you take a calculus class. The you at the end of the class hasn't 'taken over' the you from the beginning of the class. You have become a being that has the additional experience of the wisdom you gained in your studies.

Ensoulment is you realizing the wisdom and insight your soul already has; the completeness of you.

Fear

Fear is a biological reaction to change or the idea of change that typically creates the "fight or flight" response in the body, which is an adrenaline-based response to, "What do I do next?" Typically, the answer is that you run habit.

Consciously experiencing fear presents opportunities for extreme growth because it gives you the opportunity to break habitual patterns—to experience the moment rather than experiencing habit, which often involves projection of the future or bringing a memory of the past into the moment.

Fear can also be defined as the biological component of duality. It is the biological response to the belief in duality that is enacted regardless of which side of duality you're on. If you're on the side of duality that says, "This is wrong," then there's fear for survival. If you're on the side that says, "This is right," there's fear that it won't continue.

Fear and the survival instinct work together to keep you small.

Fear-based

Actions based on fear rather than conscious choice, a habitual, unconscious mentality (operating system) based on fear.

Fear-based operating system (FBOS)

You are a fear-based being. It is not something you can argue. It is a fact. Period. Full stop. End of sentence. You cannot argue with the fact that you are a fear-based being because you have been built to operate from fear in order to continue surviving. You've been built to startle at loud noises. You've been built to have the fight-or-flight response trigger in you. You've been built to be wary and aware of your surroundings. All of this can be summarized or reduced to fear. There is no need to be ashamed of admitting the fears that you find yourself experiencing because it is a core aspect of being human. You were brought into this incarnation running the fear-based operating system, meaning you're constantly experiencing the world based on fear. The survival instinct is continuously asking you to be wary. The survival instinct is continuously trying to keep you small and it has extreme measures it can go to in order to keep you from sticking your neck out, from standing out in the crowd, from being noticed. The survival instinct flares up in you and requires your habitual responses to stimulus and triggers.

As consciousness is applied to the fear-based operating system, and as you break out of habitual response patterns, you're able to experience what is going on in your life from a new perspective and shift into a consciousness-based operating system.

Fear is a choice not a mandate
A high-vibrational reaction to a fear. Watch fear occur in your life. Watch it, watch it, choose and choose again to see it a different way, to see it rather than feel it.

Your reaction to an experience is a choice and not an inevitability. Fear is a choice, and so is fascination.

Fire hose
We use this term to refer to situations where strong emotions are acted out in unconscious ways. When you "fire hose," it's as though you are "spraying" your emotions onto those around you.

We frequently see this pattern with people who are learning to set boundaries. They find themselves in a situation they want to change, but are hesitant to act. They wait to act, which causes the feelings to build to a breaking point. When they finally do set a boundary, it is often accompanied by shouting, anger, throwing things, or other intense behaviors. A boundary was set, but it was done from a low-vibrational place.

Healthy, high-vibrational, boundary setting is an extremely important part of the spiritual journey. To do this, live consciously, know the truth of you in this moment, and act upon it quickly.

Free will

Free will is the opportunity to be in amnesia about the truth of you: the truth of your infinite, immortal nature.

Free will allows you to experience Earth as YOU see fit. No one can interfere with your chosen experience—not your soul, and not even The Creator.

Note, we said your chosen experience. You choose how you experience everything. Your free will gives you this ability. Now, we are not saying that everything that happens in your life feels like something you have chosen on a personality level; however, your chosen reaction to everything that happens in your life is within your purview.

Free will gives you the option to break out of the fear-based operating system, to break habits, exercise change and choose consciousness.

Free-will zone

An experiment that was initiated by The Eloheim after being invited by The Creator to come up with something new for souls to experience. It is an opportunity for souls to incarnate in a completely amnesic state and live a lifetime through their own direction, without influence from external forces, to grow as a soul. The free-will zone is inclusive of the solar system that holds Earth.

Fulfillment

Grace, ease, and bliss; living in the physical form and running the consciousness-based operating system, while having a spiritual partnership with the soul.

Gate latch

The sound that happens when a gate swings shut and the latch hooks. When we speak with you and you come to understand a concept, we hear a gate latch sound. Sometimes, we feel the change in you and then we hear the sound.

God

A word used to describe the concept of an all-knowing Creator, but can be interpreted to mean anything. God is a word defined by the individual according to his or her experience. There is not one definition for everyone. To say the word "God" and expect others to understand what you intend to mean by that word is too open to misinterpretation. To avoid this, we recommend using at least 10 words to convey complex spiritual concepts such as "God."

Going to see the king

We use this phrase to describe your interactions with authority figures.

AN EXAMPLE:

You want to speak to your boss about a promotion. How do you approach "going to see the king"? It is essential that when you "go to see the king," or anyone else for that matter, that you bring your high-vibrational, conscious self to the encounter. Keep "What is true now?" as your focus. Remember, when you encounter an authority figure, don't let their response to you tell you who you are. Emanate the truth of you, focus on this moment, state preferences, set boundaries, and remember that it is all happening *for* you.

When you go to see the king, whomever the king is in your world, if you show up authentically you've done your part to contribute to a conscious conversation. If you encounter people who know who they are and present themselves authentically—whether it's a king or a boss or a baker—you can trust the exchange to be high-vibrational or at least conscious or at a minimum not generating more static. If they don't do their half, well, that's something very, very important to know about them, isn't it?

Going with the flow

Comment: "I'm going to go with the flow; I'll just deal with things as they come up."

Response: Be cautious about this idea. "The flow" is often a "path of least resistance," a low-vibrational energetic.

Comment: What I meant is, "I'm going to be conscious about whatever comes up."

Response: Great, say that instead. It makes a big difference. There is an energetic pattern in the idea of "going with the flow" that is a mismatch with who you are now. Saying, "I'll attend to what arises," OK, that's fine. Saying, "I'll be conscious about what shows up," OK, that's good. Saying, "I'll go with the flow." Nope. Why?

Too frequently, "going with the flow" results in you forgetting to set boundaries because the idea is, "Well, whatever happens I'll just flow with it!" This is not a recommended activity. OK OK

We are not suggesting you become rigid; we love for you to explore uncertainty! What we are recommending is that you continue to be conscious as you explore flexibility. Even if you are experiencing someone else's plans, you can still stand with the intention of observing and making choices, setting boundaries, stating preferences, and using your free will to explore your reactions to your creations.

Grace

Grace is living your life knowing that everything that is happening is happening for your growth. "I gracefully recognize this experience is here to teach me. I don't have to approach this as a victim. I can approach this as a creator." That's being in a state of grace.

Growth

Consciousness infusing the incarnation, resulting in transformation.

Guides

A generic or general term used for beings that are not currently in physical form that are available to assist those who are in physical form, through a variety of means—through channels, through coincidence, through synchronicities, through dreams, and many other ways.

Habit/Habitual response

Habit is tied into the fear of getting dead and the survival instinct. Since the body is programmed to stay alive, it will say, "Well, this hasn't killed me yet, so let's continue." Change makes the body feel like there's a potential to get killed. Change means new factors to manage, new things to deal with, and new situations to juggle. It is easier on the body if it already knows the threats that are involved in your day-to-day life and has already established that none of them are threatening enough to get you dead. The body is going to want to keep repeating that pattern. If you know that a food is poisonous to you, you don't eat it again—making that a healthy habit. But the survival instinct, as translated into 21st-century Earth, ends up looking like, "I can't quit this job that I hate because I'm too afraid of getting dead. I'm too engrained in this habit to try something else."

Hamster-wheel thinking

The habitual mind repetitiously trying to think its way out of "problems." Repetitive thinking about past and/or future experiences misses the experience of the moment.

Healing

Consciousness-infused biological responses and choices which create growth and a transformed experience of the body.

Heart–power chakra combination

From a soul's perspective, your heart chakra (4th) and power chakra (3rd) are combining. We see the energy flow as a figure-8 pattern, or an infinity symbol.

There's no longer a difference between acting from your heart chakra and acting from your power chakra. This means that you no longer go out into the world expecting to gain if others are going to lose from your actions. You no longer go out in the world knowing that you could be powerful at the expense of others. The idea of climbing over someone else to get to what you want becomes as distasteful as murder, or rape, or arson, or anything that you personally have a big problem with. You are not able to function in the world in a way that is not within your own integrity. You can't cheat a little on the side. You can't sneak down and operate from your power chakra, ignoring your heart chakra for a few hours and then expect to jump back to the heart chakra and ignore the power chakra. You can't play that game anymore. Consciousness illuminates the truth of them working in teamwork and it says there's no way you can be in the world without being from your integrity, being from your authenticity, and being from your wholeness.

Heart chakra energy has often times been out of balance—either "I serve, I love, I give," especially women, "I give, give, give,"—or your heart's closed down. There's been a lot of out-of-balance heart chakra energy on this planet.

When the power chakra gets out of balance it tends to be either "I'm going to go take care of business," with a corporate-raider kind of energy, or you have no boundaries and you're a victim.

The merging of the heart and power chakras addresses this imbalance. When you bring in the density of the power chakra and combine it with the etheric nature of the heart chakra, together they operate from a more balanced state. That's really the beauty of it.

The combined chakra can be called the ensouled chakra or the ensoulment chakra. It's the chakra where the energetic center of the body emanates out into the world.

High-vibrational

High-vibrational refers to actions, thoughts, ideas, and relationships which are based on consciousness and conscious choices. It is not a judgmental term; rather it is descriptive of the fact that your body is actually vibrating at a different rate than it did before you infused consciousness into your life.

Your soul vibrates at a very high rate. Raising your vibration by living consciously is a very important step in living from your soul's perspective and walking the path of ascension.

Hoarding

One of the most low-vibrational states you experience. "I'm going to look out for me and I don't care what happens to other people." Hoarders are constantly in lack and looking for how they can get more. They are obsessed by the question, "How can I get what I don't have?" They never feel like they have enough of what they need.

Homo spiritus

A name for a state of being that is possible when you live in collaboration with your soul incorporating your soul's perspective; a transformed, expanded experience of the physical form and a shifted paradigm of how one is on Earth.

Living from the consciousness-based operating system, pursuing the path of ascension.

Insight

Information received directly from your soul.

The challenge when explaining the word "insight" is that it is a process that uses the brain but must not be confused with "thinking."

There are a few characteristics that illuminate the differences between the two: the mind is limited and will often present limiting messages. The mind's messages are repetitive and often negative. Insight will present ideas and options you've never considered before, which are always positive and constructive in their nature. Insight will never demean you; it will never be negative and it will always be supportive of your growth and transformation.

Jackets on the coat rack

Imagine that you have a row of jackets hanging on pegs by the front door. Each of these jackets represents an emotion. Just as you can choose which jacket you want to wear when you head out into the weather, you can choose which emotion you wish to experience.

Of course, this requires practice and spiritual discipline, but it is true: Every emotion is a choice.

What jacket will you wear today?

Joy

Joy is when you experience happiness without feeling like the other shoe is going to drop. You're just happy. And as you think, "Oh, but…" you don't let the "Oh, but…" have any airtime. Uncertainty makes joy possible. When you're comfortable with uncertainty, it is possible to be in joy. When you're comfortable with uncertainty, joy is possible because you don't require the situation to be a certain way in order for you to experience happiness, and prolonged happiness is joy.

Karma

The word "karma" had a strong definition coming out of Eastern religious beliefs. When it came to the West, the term became somewhat bastardized to mean, "If you're not good, something bad is going to happen to you."

Karma had a big duality perspective in it but if you take the duality out of it, it becomes, "Everything teaches me," instead of, "I'm waiting to get punished for any mistakes or slip-ups I make."

Lack

The idea that there is not enough. Lack is a fallacy; you live in an abundant universe. Lack is a sense of, "I should have more. Something is wrong or broken here." This is experiencing your life from a victim mentality. You are a creator; everything in your life is in your life to help you grow as a soul. As a creator, if you feel a sense of "not enough," look at it as an opportunity to uncover the actual blocks to your desire. We refer to these blocks as static and baggage. Living consciously is the path to clearing these blocks and experiencing your world in its true state, the state of abundance.

Landing

Spiritual growth tends to follow this pattern: periods of intense growth followed by periods that feel more like rests. We call these "resting" times being on the landing and the "growth" times climbing the stairs.

Lateral pass

It can be tempting to want to find a way to give responsibility for your experiences to someone else. This transfer of responsibility can look like: "I turn this problem over to my angels," or "I let my higher self deal with it," or even "God, take this burden from me!"

We call this making a lateral pass.

The assumption being made in this idea is that whomever you are making the lateral pass to is actually ready, willing, and able to do anything with your creation. You are in a free-will zone; we dispute that anyone or anything is here to take away your "problems" or that anyone or anything is better suited to interact with your creation than you are.

You created it so that you could learn from it. Why would you want to give it away? Does it feel too "hard" to deal with on your own? Ok, that's why we have lots of tools to help you interact with your creations in new ways and from new perspectives. You are not alone in your exploration, but you are solely responsible for how you choose to react to your creations.

Layers of the onion

A quick way of saying that while issues may come up again and again, you are experiencing them at a deeper level each time.

Learning

As an incarnate soul, the processes that you go through in order to have the growth you desire are called "learning." The journey is a journey of change, shifts, transformation, and ascension, which is all brought into the physical system through the process of internal and external transformation, a reflection of all of the learning that has occurred.

Light worker

A soul incarnating at this time with the specific desire to grow spiritually and live consciously. A person walking the path of ascension. A Homo sapiens desiring to live as Homo spiritus.

Low-vibrational

A state of being that comes from living in the fear-based operating system, not looking for conscious understanding or an experience of the dynamics being presented to you. Living habitually rather than opening to new experience.

It is not a judgmental term; rather, it is descriptive of the fact that your body is actually vibrating at a different rate than it would if you infused consciousness into your life.

Your soul vibrates at a very high rate. It is difficult to connect to your soul's energy when living a low-vibrational life.

Marble sculpture

In a sense, bliss is inside of you. It's like Michelangelo carving a sculpture. The marble block is there; the sculpture is inside the block, not yet revealed. When you are in habit, you are looking at the block and thinking, "This could be more, this could be more, but that would require getting the tools out, it would require doing a lot of work, it would require, it would require…" and you find reasons not to change. Habit keeps you from seeing the beauty of the finished sculpture. All you get is the plain block. Now, if you want to get more out of your life, if you want to be that finished sculpture, the excess marble has to come off.

Just as the act of chipping away marble reveals the sculpture underneath, the act of attending to triggers and static reveals the highest version of you. When Michelangelo chipped a piece off the marble block, he didn't have to chip that same piece again; however, you often you have to go deeper and deeper and deeper in the same part of the block. That we know. But it is not that you do some work and then you have to do that work again. It's that you do some work and then sometimes you'll revisit that area to do deeper, finer work.

Sometimes, you've been working on the front and you haven't looked at the back in two years. And you turn the block around and you say, "Oh Lord, I'm really not attending to these things back here, am I? Well, I'm going to. I'm going to attend to them now. There were opportunities to look at this stuff before and I didn't, but I'm going to look at them now; in this moment, the current version of me is going to look at them now. I'm going to use my tools and take this opportunity to offer a different emanation and to transform static and triggers as I go."

You're clearing away the old rectangular-shaped block to reveal the beautiful figure that's always been there, just waiting for the accurate and consistent application of the appropriate tools to illuminate the beauty that only needed you to be willing to do the steps that unearth it, unveil it. You are there. You are the sculptor. And the consistency that you are willing to apply to the project tells the story. It allows the unfoldment.

The sculptor doesn't *build* the marble statue, it's something that's *revealed*—and that's what you're doing. You're revealing the integrity of you, meaning your soul expressed through the physical form, and the only way to reveal it is to remove that which isn't of the integrity of you.

It's the process of chipping and filing and buffing away the unwanted sections that reveals the sculpture. Being angry that the sculpture doesn't appear full-formed is ridiculous. When you find yourself in trigger or static—frustration, anger, anxiety, memories that trouble you—remember this idea that the sculpture doesn't show up fully formed. It's the journey of the discovery of the sculpture that is the meaningful part. When the sculpture is placed someplace in public and it emanates its beauty, then others get to experience it.

It does not get created until someone stands there and says, "I'm willing. I'm willing to chip off this section; I'm willing to buff this part out. I'm willing to scratch my head and wonder, 'Do I want an arm here or not?' I am willing." Your willingness to look at your static and triggers creates the beauty of you, which can then be emanated for an eternity. You have the marble block; you can be angry at it for not being finished or you can put your stamp on it. You can make it the vision you have. And then that vision will be emanated into the universe forever.

Stand in front of your unfinished self and decide what bits you want to keep and what bits you want to get rid of. Just as Michelangelo had the variety of tools that he used, you have tools to help you chip away the things you don't wish to see anymore. At some point you can stand there and say, "Comparing me to me, I have an arm now. Last year that was just a block but now you can actually see the fingers. You can see that I've decided how I want to be."

Math problem

If we ask: "What's 9,897,209.5 times 8,239,203?" you wouldn't take the first number that comes to mind as the right answer, but you'll take the first emotion that comes in as an indisputably correct position. If you find yourself in an emotion that doesn't seem actually relevant to the moment, be kind to yourself about it. Just remind yourself, "Oh yeah, that's right, the first emotion that trips along isn't necessarily the one I want to run with."

You can let yourself have the emotion, but know why you're having it. If all of a sudden, you feel sad or upset and you don't know why you're feeling that way, ask yourself, "Is there any good reason to be having this emotion? And if there isn't, then what can I ascertain about the state I'm in?" Remind yourself, "This emotion has no basis in reality, in the reality of this moment. This emotion is a choice."

Mind

The mind's thoughts and insight are both processed by the brain. The mind is only capable of taking the spiritual journey so far. At some point, the mind's ability to manage the spiritual journey comes to a standstill. Without the infusion of insight from the soul, the journey will stagnate. When you act, react, and create only from your mind, you're cutting yourself off from the vast resources of your soul and the Akashic Records. In this context, it's easy to see that allowing the mind to run the incarnation is limiting.

Mob mentality

Matching energy with low-vibrational states or low-vibrational people. Going with the flow. Acting habitually, as part of a group.

Money flows, not grows

Money flows, it doesn't grow. In the past, a lot of people have made their fortunes just by letting their money grow, but that was an old paradigm. Have you looked at interest rates lately? It doesn't work that way anymore, does it? Part of the reason for this change is the energetic truth of money is being revealed: high-vibrational money *flows*, it doesn't grow.

Money flows where consciousness goes! Become more conscious of your relationship to money by using the money mantra: *I am in financial* **flow**, *money comes to me in infinite ways.*

Mt. Everest

A quick and easy way to remind yourself that you do hard stuff on purpose all the time. Climbing Mount Everest is hard, but people climb it. And they do it on purpose, right? Learning another language—for most of you that's really hard but you do it. On purpose. You want to learn to play an instrument. It's challenging, but you do it. On purpose. And then you wonder, "Why is my spiritual life and my spiritual development so hard?" Somehow the difficulty of spiritual development is interpreted as you being a victim of your spiritual path. You are a creator. You are choosing your reactions to your creation. Therefore, take responsibility for your experience and approach it in a new way. Allow yourself to respond with the attitude of, "Yes, this is hard, but I choose it. Just like I choose to climb up a tall mountain or I choose to learn another language, or I choose to learn how to dance ballet. I choose to do hard things all the time. I choose growth and transformation."

On the bus

A cute way of expressing the idea that you are committed to a specific path or idea. We commonly use it to indicate that you are committed to the path of ascension.

Overachieving light worker

A playful description used to illuminate when light workers start thinking, "I have to keep pushing, pushing, pushing to get to that outcome." This is doing rather than being. It is very common to apply the "doing" mentality to the spiritual journey. Part of spiritual transformation is healing this habit.

When you are playing with the overachieving light worker idea, it is all about winning, getting an A+, getting a gold star, being first in line, being on the bus, getting to ascension as fast as you possibly can. In this, there is the risk of losing sight of the fact that "now" is the end result, is the goal, is the desire, is the point of it all. "Now," what you're doing right now, is it.

Peace

Peace is the experience of you being non-disturbable. It is the idea that no matter what's going on you know what your center is. You know the truth of you and you don't resist it. You can have peace even with things you hate about yourself if you don't resist the truth of you being present. Peace is: "No matter what's going on, I'm still me. No matter who's triggering me, I'm still me."

Personality

The aspect of the incarnate human that has a name, that has preferences, that has a history, that has a future, that has relationships. It's the aspect of you that's currently under development.

The power of the personality is that it wields free will. Therefore, the personality actually is completely in charge of the incarnation by controlling whether or not consciousness is employed, deciding how to react to situations, and deciding whether or not to pursue ascension.

Power

When you live in scarcity—the feeling of lack, fear, guilt, and unconscious low vibration—one of the most popular ways to cope is to exert, or believe you can exert, power over others. The sense that you control another's destiny provides a (false) sense of certainty about one's self.

Control and power do not create safety. Control and power simply require more and more control and power. It's a never-ending cycle.

The only thing to seek power over is power over your habits. The only person you can actually control is yourself; use free will to choose to change.

Proof

Proof is the repeated demand for certainty, the demand for your eyes to see it in order for you to believe it. Proof is the biggest barrier between you and living an expanded sense of yourself, because the need for proof comes from the small mind. "Prove it to me" is a defiant statement of unconsciousness. Thus it is one of our least-favorite terms because it's so deeply ingrained in the victim mentality. It doesn't have any belief in creatorship or the ability to open to new possibilities without certainty being promised. Your soul's perspective will illuminate many things that can't be proven to the small mind. Will you let the habit of needing proof result in you missing out on these new experiences?

Protect what's mine

This is all about the idea that there's not enough for everyone. It's the notion that, whatever you have, you must make sure no one gets it. You must ensure that you will always have enough. This fallacy is twofold. One, that there's not enough for everyone, and two, that if you have it, it will be enough. It's the idea that if you have enough food set aside, you'll always have food—but eventually, that food gets used, eaten, spoiled, and then there's never enough. It comes from the perspective of lack and the dreaded "h" word—hoarding—which is one of the lowest-vibrational words you have.

Safety

The idea that you can control outcomes. Safety is sought by looking for certainty. Certainty is a fallacy—it can never be achieved. Everything has some degree of uncertainty in it. The survival instinct constantly pushes you to seek safety; the fear-based operating system gives you no way to get there. The ascension journey helps you learn that the only sense of true safety comes from a deep connection to your soul and moving moment to moment through clarity.

Sandpaper/Sandpaper people

A metaphor for the way triggers and fears can be viewed as opportunities for change and growth the way sandpaper shapes a piece of wood: an opportunity to smooth your edges.

Sandpaper people describes relationships that give you an opportunity to grow and transform, typically in an uncomfortable way.

It is never used to indicate victimhood, but rather is a reminder to be conscious that the person or situation is there for your growth.

Serenity

The experience of, "I don't have to seek outside of myself for completeness." A state that has no opposite.

Service mentality

The mistaken idea that you should put another's journey before yours; believing your needs are secondary to others' needs; the idea that "doing good in the world" comes before caring for yourself.

The most powerful way you can be in the world is by loving yourself well and then walking your life from the place of loving yourself well. When you love yourself well, you give the greatest gift you have to give, and that is emanating your uniqueness. Until you love yourself well, you're not really giving a gift. You're simply doing. You're doing and doing and doing in the world. But there's no flavor. There's no taste.

Healthy service is asking, "How can I emanate the highest possible vibration?"

If you choose to offer yourself in service, the first step is to ask your soul for insight, "What is it that best serves me in serving others, in offering myself to others? What serves me first, where will I grow the most?" You want to be in the most conscious frame of mind possible in order to interact at the highest vibrational level possible. Your emanation is your true gift.

Through the act of loving yourself, you give the gift of the truth of you to this world. There is no truth of you until it includes loving yourself. It doesn't exist. "Empty calories" is a way to say it.

We see folks putting themselves out there in the world, saying, "I want everyone to feel better, to feel happier, to have more, to be in a good space." The idea is that taking care of everyone else first is going to be the path to your own bliss, your own peace, your own joy. We have not seen this work well long-term.

People who live to serve others appear energetically drained because their own needs have not been precious to them. They're missing the core amount of attention, of rest, of nourishment, of peace, of quiet, of meditation, of walking, or dancing, whatever it is that feeds them as a person and keeps them whole. Folks in service mentality have been letting pieces of those things go to other people because they think, "Well, if they're happy, I'll be happy, or at least I won't be so distracted by their needs."

The path out of this is to set boundaries. Boundaries don't mean: "I don't love you anymore." Boundaries mean: "I have to love myself first so I have extra love to give. I can't give from this place. I have to give from a whole place." If you keep giving from weakness, eventually you will have nothing left. If you set boundaries, you will rejuvenate yourself.

Unhealthy service mentality can be highly triggered when there are large "disasters." You see something on the news and you think, "Oh my God, those people, they don't have any place to live." You look in your checkbook and you send off whatever you can send off and you think, "I wish I could do more." If you feel that your money, time, or skills are the only way to "serve," then you will often be frustrated. Remember, healthy service is asking, "How can I emanate the highest possible vibration?"

Investing in your energetic and raising your vibration is really the way you meet your desire to help the world. The key here is that you realize that as you raise your vibration and live more consciously, your awareness of others' needs will expand yet your ability to physically interact with their needs will not. Use your free will to decide where you want to physically interact with others. How you manage your reaction to the areas where you are aware of the needs of others, yet cannot physically interact with them, is a spiritual challenge best handled by becoming more conscious, which raises your vibration and increases your emanation.

It may be tempting to be so overwhelmed by the many "problems" in the world that you do nothing, including work on yourself. We remind you, emanating your truth into the world is powerfully transformative. That's the greatest gift you can give to yourself and to the world.

Shadow

The aspects of yourself that you don't want anybody else to know about; the things that you are ashamed of and deny, and repress; places where you don't love yourself yet, parts of you that you reject as unacceptable, wrong, bad, or even evil; aspects of your life you feel are socially unacceptable yet still true; honest experiences that you have had that you didn't handle with consciousness; shame: these from your shadow.

We see your shadow aspects as dark holes or gray areas in your energy body that make you look a bit like Swiss cheese.

Our desire is to help you love all parts of yourself, which allows you to live from the soul's perspective as a Homo spiritus being.

Shake shoulders

Demanding attention, insisting that you be listened to, trying to change someone, needing people to agree with you so you will feel safe. The accompanying visual is that you are shaking someone by the shoulders and preaching to them. You may not actually do that, but energetically that's what's going on.

Soul

The infinite, immortal nature of your true self, including the collection of every lifetime you've had on Earth, the time between lifetimes, every lifetime you've had in other incarnational opportunities, and all other experiences.

The soul is a vast reservoir of experience and an eternally curious being.

Animating a human body does not require the entirety of your soul. There is no way you can stuff an entire soul into a human body. But there's a percentage of your soul that has been allocated to be experience-able in this lifetime.

Soulmate

Humans desire safety, and typically believe they need something outside themselves to be safe. That search for something outside of themselves is 'spiritualized' to become "soulmate." The idea is that, "There's another soul out there that is destined to complete me; then I will feel safe." The truth is that all souls reflect the completeness of the creation. No one soul is more able to complete you than any other because that's just not how it works. You are a complete being experiencing the physical life.

That said, because you incarnate in soul groups, there can be souls that you are more familiar with and can feel more connected to simply through familiarity and decisions made in pre-birth planning to share certain experiences. But the quest for a soulmate to complete you is a great, great spiritual fallacy. The quest for a human to partner with or to spend time with in order to facilitate growth is a completely different matter. It can also be a friend, parent, lover, dog, cat, or anything that facilitates spiritual growth. Everything can be used by the incarnate human to facilitate growth, but no one person is specifically sent here to complete you.

So, if soulmate is perceived as someone who is going to complete you, we don't buy into that. But if soulmate is perceived as someone who is going to facilitate your growth, who may or may not stick around for a long time in your life, then that's a more healthy way to use that term. But we advise not using it at all. The implication is that somehow you're not fully you unless this person comes along, and that's lack.

Soul's perspective

The wisdom of your soul incorporated into your experience of being human. It's the insight available to you when you live from the consciousness-based operating system.

From the soul's perspective, there is no judgment, no duality, no fear about life in the physical form. Everything is fascinating.

Your soul knows this is all just a journey in learning. There's no right, there's no wrong, there's no good, there's no bad. It's a journey in learning, exploration, experience. It's not the destination—it's the journey.

Spirituality

Functioning from more than just the survival instinct. Awareness of and openness to experiences outside of those that are "provable" or "repeatable." Knowledge that you are more than just this human form.

Spiritual discipline

When you think, "I don't feel good in this environment," spiritual discipline says, "This is hard, but I'm going to do it." It's challenging, right? You use your spiritual choice and you consciously work with an experience that you wish to change. It's spiritual discipline to align free will with the desire for evolutionary change, and to persevere. Choose and choose again for the growth you desire.

Spiritual growth

Another term for transformation and learning, indicating that your learning is not based on your mind or habits but on consciousness-based transformation.

Static

Unconscious reactions and thoughts; coping mechanisms, masks, lies, baggage, dishonesty, hiding from your authentic expression or the completeness of you; anything that interrupts your ability to stay in the authentic truth of the moment. The mind, the survival instinct, the body, and fear all generate static to keep you small.

Static includes all the reasons you have sold yourself on which you use to avoid presenting the truth of you to the world. It will crop up more intensely as you start to recognize the greatness and the vastness of your true self.

Living consciously is the path to clearing static.

Suffering

Suffering occurs when you experience the world from a victim mentality—not believing you are a creator and instead living in limitation and habit.

You've all suffered, and you have the choice in the suffering to experience it as learning. No matter what is occurring, there's always that choice. Change happens. What is, is. Let's look at it from a new perspective. Do you want to climb out of this new experience with something learned from it, or do you want to wallow in what happened to you, in victimhood?

Survival Instinct

A body-based dynamic that puts the continuation of life at the top of the list of importance. The survival instinct serves you deeply by continuing life even when physical, mental, or emotional experiences lead you to feeling as though you want your life to end.

There had to be a survival instinct put into the system because duality is so different from your experience of being a soul that it would be very tempting to "drop one toe into this water" and then run away. The body's innate survival instinct keeps you in the incarnation long enough to be able to make conscious choices about the experience.

In order to live a conscious life, one must transform one's relationship to the survival instinct. Consciousness asks you to make steps toward change that the survival instinct will be resistant to embrace because to the body, any change feels like potential death and therefore, should be avoided at all costs.

The survival instinct is one of your greatest treasures as well as one of the most challenging places to transform with consciousness because it's so deeply based in the body, and based in unconscious processing. When you are able to consciously modify the way the survival instinct works in the incarnation, you open yourself up to a deep and profound way of re-experiencing how it is to be human. This is one of the major steps in living as Homo spiritus, as an ascended being.

Thinking

The process by which the brain exerts control over the incarnation.

The survival instinct is often the driving force behind thinking.

Thinking is often employed to avoid experiencing change, transformation, or growth. In the spiritual journey, transforming your thought process with consciousness to choose insight from your soul rather than small-mind thinking is one of the major steps to becoming an ascended being.

The brain is the thinking organ. The mind is the thought process. Insight, which comes from your soul, can feel like thinking, however, the content will clarify if you are thinking or receiving insight.

Time

A body-based system by which control is exerted over the incarnation to try to calm the survival instinct into belief that certainty is possible. Time, the passage of time, and the knowledge of when things should be done and how they should be done, helps to make the body feel as though correct, safe, and/or secure action is taking place.

When you recognize that you are living from insight from your soul, from one "aha" to the next, you will no longer need "time" to make you feel safe. You will live in one expanded moment. How that one expanded moment will interact with the turning of the planet and the change of the seasons is a glorious exploration that we anticipate will keep you entertained and enchanted for what you would refer to, in time, as many years.

When you remove time as a controlling factor, what you perceive as time—or changes over time—becomes a tapestry you weave rather than the master with the whip telling you how to live.

Tools

Techniques used to interrupt the unconscious running of habit by using consciousness to shift out of a fear-based operating system into the consciousness-based operating system. See the table of contents for a list of tools included in this book.

Transformation

A term describing change, especially change along the ascension process.

Triggers

Triggers are stimuli that the personality experiences which bring up opportunities to explore unhealed parts of the personality self.

Triggers are handholds

Triggers are the handholds on the climbing wall of ascension. Triggers are not to be avoided or run from. Triggers are to be embraced as opportunities for progress. Now, we understand that triggers have made you spin and suffer, and it's very hard to see them as an opportunity, but's still true; triggers are handholds on the climbing wall of ascension.

When you contemplate climbing up one of those climbing walls—you all have seen these walls with the different places to put your hands and your feet—you see the next handhold and you think, "Ok, I think I can make it to that one, I think I can reach that one," you're grateful that handhold is there because that handhold takes you up to where you want to go. This is how we would like you to look at fear, guilt, lack, anger, and other low-vibrational states; look at them as though they are a handhold on a climbing wall. Because that's what they are; they're the way you get where you want to go.

When a fear comes up, grab it with both hands and say, "Thank you for being here. I need this handhold. I want you here so I can grow. I put healing above all else. I want ascension. I'm going to the top of whatever this thing is. I'm going to make you a handhold." Seize them with the same intensity, gratitude, and upliftment that that next handhold would give you if you were climbing a mountain.

When you get to the top, all the transformed triggers are the foundation under your feet. You see? You climb and you climb and you transform and you transform and then you get to the top and what do you do? You get to look out at the view. You get to see a new perspective. All of a sudden there's a vista. But that vista is only possible because of the experiences that lifted you up that wall. All those handholds, all those triggers, all those places where you slipped a little bit, they all helped you become the new you.

Unconscious

Acting from the fear-based operating system without the intervention of consciousness; running habit.

Understanding is overrated

You've been taught that "understanding" is a worthy goal. You use your amazing brain to "wrap your mind around" something until you understand it. We say "understanding is overrated" to remind you that understanding something with your mind isn't the only way you can interact with it. There is a vast amount of insight from your soul that you can access on any subject. Reminding yourself that "understanding is overrated" will help you break the habit of limited thinking and remember to open to your soul's perspective.

If thinking could have solved it, it would have solved it long ago because you sure have thought about it enough! Open to insight and add your soul's perspective to the mix.

Unfolding

While you're in the process of transformation, it unfolds like a rose opening; you never quite know what the next step is going to be, just like you never know what the next petal of the rose is going to look like until it opens and unfolds. On your unique journey, you experience something that's never been experienced before—the unfolding truth of you which is gradually revealed as you walk the path of consciousness.

Vibration

Low VIBRATION: A state of being that comes from living from the fear-based operating system, not looking for conscious understanding or experience of the dynamics being presented to you. Living habitually rather than opening to new experience.

It is not a judgmental term, rather it is descriptive of the fact that your body is actually vibrating at a different rate than it would if you infused consciousness into your life.

Your soul vibrates at a very high rate. It is difficult to connect to your soul's energy when living a low-vibrational life.

HIGH-VIBRATION: A description of actions, thoughts, ideas, and relationships which are based on consciousness and conscious choices. It is not a judgmental term, rather it is descriptive of the fact that your body is actually vibrating at a different rate than it did before you infused consciousness into your life.

Your soul vibrates at a very high rate. Raising your vibration by living consciously is a very important step in living from your soul's perspective and walking the path of ascension.

Victim/Victimhood

The mistaken perspective that things happen to you that you are at the whim of any other creature, being, person, or eventuality that you experience while on Earth. Running the fear-based operating system. It is a perspective that is very easy to assume because you incarnate with amnesia, making it difficult for you to remember your infinite nature, or the fact that you planned to be here and have the experiences you are having.

When events trigger you or you have experiences that you deem negative, your reaction is, "Why did this happen to me?" which is a victim's perspective. With a conscious journey and a conscious life, you're able to start seeing the world as the creator that you are, and start asking, "Why is this happening *for* me?" and realizing that "Everything teaches me something."

Woman by the campfire

We use this phrase as a quick way to describe the following energetic: "If my man doesn't come home to me, I die." This energetic is part of your DNA, it's in your cells, it's part of your culture, but primarily it comes from alternate expressions where this was much more of a reality: If your man took the meat from his hunt to *her* fire instead of yours, you and your kids could literally starve to death.

It's also a shortcut way of saying, "I am hard-wired to believe something that I haven't consciously explored."

As you shift out of Homo sapiens into Homo spiritus one of the major differences between the two states is understanding the influence you have, using consciousness, over the biological reactions as presented by the body doing its normal job. Just as the body keeps breathing and the heart keeps beating and the blood keeps moving and all that stuff keeps happening, habits keep getting thrown up in front of you. Not just the habit of fear, but the idea of lack, the idea of safety, the idea of security, abundance all these issues that you've habituated that are part of your biology.

Biological reactions to stimulus that previously haven't been run through consciousness are now coming under your influence. As you move out of the Homo sapiens mindset into the Homo spiritus experience it becomes your responsibility to consciously monitor the biological reactions to stimulus. You're responsible for the emanations you create as you react.

This includes pain, emotional stimulus, memory stimulus, and fear stimulus. All of these things that you previously felt were hardwired in you can become the purview of your conscious exploration.

Your internal world creates your external journey

Your internal world is the creation point for the external expression of your life. Not the other way around. Your internal process is projected on the movie screen of your external life where it all plays out. This allows you to learn and grow from the experience of observing your internal life projected (externalized).

Your internal world is a series of choices that you've made, even if the choice was to default to a habitual pattern, to default to a culturally driven pattern, to default to the childhood pattern. Those are still choices.

Remember, it can't happen in your external world unless it's true in your internal world. When experiences arise, ask, "What are you showing me about me? What are you telling me about me?" Let the experiences inform you rather than staying with the surface reaction of, "They're just triggering me or challenging me or frustrating me or driving me bananas." Ask instead, "What are you showing me about me?"

You can't dictate how people react to you, necessarily, but you can certainly influence the outcome by loving yourself well and sending that into the world instead of doubt and anguish and anxiety and feeling stepped on and being a victim and all that. If you walk into a room knowing you love yourself and emanating your truth, you're going to have a different experience than if you walk into a room feeling like a victim and a doormat. You will be known and reacted to by the way you love yourself.

Your awareness of your internal world becomes so rich and well-developed, so well-known and mapped by you, that your emanation of the truth of your internal world starts to resemble a fountain that bubbles up and spills over without stopping. It's not something you have to think about or work yourself through or get going. It bubbles up in you and it spills over, just like a fountain does, the fullness of your internal world emanating out into the world. This doesn't involve you acting in the world as much as it involves you experiencing the world from your truth. The truth of you being real.

What is channeling?

Channeling is a process where I set my personality aside to allow Eloheim and The Council to use my physical form to convey their teachings.

PLEASE NOTE: This is not possession. It only occurs when I give explicit permission. I can stop it at ANY time.

When I am channeling I feel as though I am standing or sitting behind and to the left of my actual body. I am aware of what is being said as the session unfolds, although I don't always remember everything that is discussed.

Eloheim and The Council specialize in reading the energy of a question, situation, or person. They often experience visual representations of the energy they sense. When this occurs, I see it as a "movie" in my head not unlike what happens when I am dreaming.

I have created a YouTube video with more details about the process. You can find it by searching YouTube for "Introduction Eloheim and The Council."

Who are Eloheim and The Council?

On February 11, 1997, I had a reading by a very skilled psychic and channel. During that reading he said that I would become a channel myself. Although I valued much of what he shared, my reaction to that statement was, YEAH, RIGHT!

I was quite familiar with channeling. I found it incredibly valuable. I just didn't see myself doing it!

That all changed when I came to Sonoma. I was invited to a friend's home to do a Lakshmi puja. The chanting left me in a very altered state. When we finished, we sat in a circle on the floor. I told one of the participants I had a message for her and then shared information she found very helpful. At the end of the sharing I said, "We are the Eloheim and we are pleased to have been with you today."

Now, even though I knew what had happened, I was overwhelmed by it and started to cry. It didn't feel bad or wrong, just very intense. It made me feel very conspicuous. I immediately told myself, "That's never going to happen again."

It was some time before it did. Over time, I got more comfortable with the idea of being a channel but I had no idea how to do it! I tried to work with Eloheim on my own once or twice. I even recorded a very useful message about habitual response on November 26, 2000, yet it just wasn't coming together. Almost two years passed without much forward movement.

Finally, a friend and I figured it out. What was needed was a second person to ask the questions and help me with the logistics of the whole thing.

In the very beginning while channeling, I had to raise my right hand in order to receive the energies (boy, am I glad that I don't have to do that any longer). I would get very thirsty, but I wasn't able to hold a glass (I still have a bunch of straws in a drawer from those days). I had a TON of insecurity about "Am I making this up?" and "Is this real?" and "Am I doing it right?" I needed a lot of reassurance just to stick with it. I would get very sleepy afterward and sometimes needed help just getting around. I had to eat a lot of protein to keep my energy level up.

Details, details, details. All of which felt completely unmanageable to me alone, but became possible once I had help.

After about one month, Eloheim told us that this wasn't just for the two of us and to get a group together. That was September 2002, when we began our weekly Eloheim sessions. We still hold meetings every Wednesday night and one Sunday per month. You can join us live or tune into our webcasts. For more information, please visit: eloheim.com/web-casts.

I had never heard the term Eloheim until they introduced themselves that way. Someone then told me it was one of the names of God. I looked it up on the Internet and found that to be true. It is important to note that although it is common to see the spelling Elohim, I was guided to use the spelling Eloheim.

Eloheim has made it clear that just as not everyone named John is the same, to not assume that all entities using the name Eloheim or Elohim are the same. The material they present with me is internally consistent and can be taken as a whole.

Eloheim is a group entity that presents with one voice. That one voice feels like a male energy. We refer to the Eloheim as "he" or "they."

They refer to themselves as "we."

Starting on June 10, 2009, I began channeling the rest of The Council. Here are the dates of their first appearances:

The Visionaries - 06/10/2009

The Guardians - 12/02/2009

The Girls - 01/06/2010

The Matriarch - 02/03/2010

The Warrior - 03/17/2010

Fred - 06/30/2010

For more information about Eloheim and The Council, please visit: eloheim.com/who-is-eloheim

What is it like to channel Eloheim and The Council?

Eloheim:

I have been channeling Eloheim since 2002. They are very easy to channel. I've channeled them while riding in a car, in a room full of playing puppies, in a haunted winery, on the radio, during an earthquake (briefly), and in all sorts of other places. They are the only Council member who I channel with eyes open. Perhaps someday other Council members will be ready for eyes open, but at this time they are all still getting used to interacting with the body and the additional stimulus of eyes open would be too much—for me and for them.

Visionaries (first channeled on 06/10/2009):

The Visionaries were the first to join Eloheim on the Council. After seven years of working with Eloheim, it was strange to imagine channeling another group. Little did I know it was just the beginning! Here are some of my comments from the first time I channeled the Visionaries:

They sat right on the edge of the chair. They are even louder than Eloheim. They use language differently and have a different cadence to their speech. I found my jaw moving in strange ways to accommodate this.

Nowadays, the Visionaries continue to be intense, but I am much more comfortable with their energy. I frequently wonder how they can say so many words in such a short period of time. They are the most rigid of the Council members and often seem to have their entire talk planned out ahead of time. To watch video from their first appearance, please visit this page on my website: http://eloheim.com/1064/eloheim-the-visionaries/.

Guardians (first channeled on 12-02-2009):

When the Guardians first came in, they had a very hard time talking. However, they sure could MOVE energy. They continue to focus on working energetically with us although they can talk easily now. A lot of what I experience when channeling the Guardians is sensing the energy they are picking up in the room. There are sometimes visuals associated with the energy, but it is more often a sense of knowing rather than seeing.

Watch their first video on this page: http://eloheim.com/1792/eloheim-3rd-and-4th-chakras-emotions-guardians-and-visionaries/.

The Girls (first channeled on 01-06-2010):

I just found this quote from my first blog posting about the Girls, "The Girls immediately sat back in the chair, got comfortable, crossed my legs, and settled in for a chat." That pretty much sums it up. They come in and chat with us. They are very comfortable with the body and very easy to channel. They have a light energy which is quite fun for me to experience. Watch their first video on this page: http://eloheim.com/2000/eloheim-10610/.

The Matriarch (first channeled on 02-03-2010:

I don't really remember much from the first time I channeled the Matriarch. Mostly I remember being sort of overwhelmed by the idea that we were *still* adding new groups to the channeling. I wasn't all that keen about the idea. However, the Matriarch is amazing to channel. Sometimes my heart opens so much that it feels like the entire room is inside of me. I feel loved and embraced by her. I am so happy she closes out our meetings. It is a wonderful energy to conclude the meeting with. You can watch her first appearance here: http://eloheim.com/2197/eloheim-audio-from-2-3-10-meeting/.

The Warrior (first channeled on 03-17-2010):

The Warrior was really hard to channel the first time. It took me six days to feel like myself again. I couldn't watch the video or listen to the audio without their energy coming back into my body and I just couldn't manage it. When they first came in, it felt like my entire body grew by two inches and then snapped back to its normal size. I was sore from head to toe the next morning. It was a strange time. Now, I have a total crush on the Warrior. I don't have a "favorite"—really I don't—but it's tempting! I get a bonus when I channel the Warrior. It is as though I am watching a movie when they tell their stories. My eyes are closed, but I see a complete, full-color movie in my head. I don't get anything like that from any of the other Council members. It's really cool. Here is video from the Warrior's second appearance: http://eloheim.com/2529/eloheim-this-is-a-choice-the-warrior-and-more-3-24-10/.

Fred (first channeled on 06-30-2010):

Fred is a total trip. I still don't think I "get" him. He carries a Galactic energy which is really huge, but very non-physical. Weird…it's weird and hard to explain. He took quite a while to figure out how to interact with the body. He's getting much better now. Fred is the opposite of the Visionaries. The Visionaries come in with a plan, Fred seems to not have a clue what he wants to talk about until the second he starts talking! People just love Fred and have powerful reactions to him. He gets more fan mail than any of the others! I have a suspicion that Fred will end up rocking my world. However, he mostly just confuses me at this point. You can watch his first video here: http://eloheim.com/3275/eloheim-and-the-full-council-fred-joins-us-6-30-10/.

Overall, channeling the Council is a very enjoyable experience. There have been plenty of times when I was practically non-functional the day after a meeting, but that seems to have passed. I learned that if I eat something really salty—popcorn works well—after a meeting, I usually feel fine the next day.

About the author

Veronica Torres: is based in Sonoma, CA. She has channeled Eloheim since 2002, both in public and private sessions. Her public channeling sessions are offered five times per month. These sessions are broadcast live on the Internet and archived for on-demand viewing.

Veronica's career history is interesting and varied, with work including: talk radio host, Rock and Roll memorabilia store owner, Network Director of a Holistic Practitioner's Group, Producer of Well Being Expos, and jewelry designer!

Photo credit: nancikerby.com

Contact

Website: eloheim.com

Facebook: facebook.com/eloheim

Twitter: twitter.com/channelers

YouTube: youtube.com/eloheimchannel

Join our live channeling sessions in person or online:
eloheim.com/web-casts

Visit our meeting archives for video and audio recordings of past gatherings:
eloheim.com/eloheim-recordings

Join our mailing list:
tinyurl.com/eloheimlist

Private session with Eloheim:
eloheim.com/meeting-schedule-private-sessions/

Preview other Eloheim books

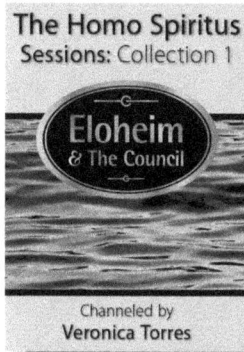

COLLECTION ONE of the Homo Spiritus Sessions includes the transcripts of EIGHT Eloheim and The Council channeling sessions held between July 7, 2010 and August 25, 2010.

The focus of COLLECTION ONE is:

It's not WHY is this happening? It's WOW this is happening! Experiences are here to facilitate growth, expansion, and transformation. Nothing happens TO you, it all happens FOR you. You create your reality by choosing your reactions to your experiences.

The spiritual journey is a natural process of expansion (growth) and contraction (contemplation). Through this process, you discover the truth of you and learn to emanate that truth into the world. Empower yourself by discerning the difference between vulnerability and weakness. Evolve your relationship to the survival instinct; don't let fear and habits tell you who you are!

The truth of you is emanated into the world through your choices about how you react to your creations. If issues come up again, it doesn't mean you're broken, it means you're going deeper; allow yourself to go deeper with it.

Feelings are not emotions! Feelings are a deep and powerful pathway to ascension based on what is actually occurring in this moment. Emotions are habitually, biologically, and/or culturally based. Be vulnerable. Tell the truth. Be honest about your feelings. Be willing to admit when you want to learn something. Open to the fact that you don't know everything.

When you're tempted to be in the past or the future, we invite you to say: "Am I courageous enough to be with me now? Am I courageous enough to attend to my concerns about me? My fascination about me. My insight about me. Am I courageous enough to do that?"

Where do you feel unlovable? The answer is the doorway to the next level of your spiritual growth. The true nature of your infinite, and immortal self resides just a breath away in any moment, and it exists for you to access at any time.

The *Homo Spiritus Sessions* series offers channeled messages from Eloheim and The Council.

The Council is comprised of seven different groups: The Guardians, The Girls, The Visionaries, The Matriarch, The Eloheim, The Warrior, and Fred. During a channeling session, each of The Council members take turns sharing their teachings. Each Council member has a distinct personality, style of delivery, and focus.

The Council is best known for their multitude of practical tools, which support our journey out of the fear-based operating system into the consciousness-based operating system.

COLLECTION ONE includes 29 tools:

Big toe, left elbow; Choose and choose again; Color with all the crayons; Don't be mean to yourself; Equal signs; Feelings are not emotions; Feet under shoulders; Go to the bathroom; How ridiculous does it have to get?; Mad Scientist; Money mantra; Neutral observation; "No" is a complete sentence; Point fingers; Preferences/ Judgments; Re-queue; Script holding; Short, factual statements; Velcro; Vulnerability vs. weakness; What is in your lap?; What is IS; What is true now?; Where am I lying to myself?; Who answers the door?; Why, why, why?; Wow!, not why?; You can't have change without change; You to you (compare).

Additionally, COLLECTION ONE includes 126 definitions of terms and concepts.

Each of the *Homo Spiritus Sessions* books can stand alone, but taken together will allow the reader to follow along with the progression of the teachings including the introduction, in-depth explanation, and evolution of The Council's tools.

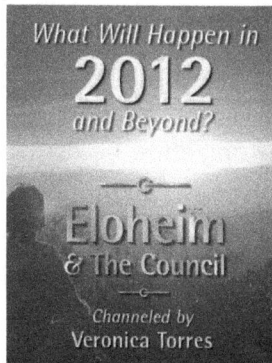

What Will Happen in 2012 and Beyond?

The question, "What will happen in 2012?" is being asked by a great many people. The Mayan calendar ends on December 21, 2012 which has given rise to a considerable amount of speculation about what might happen, including predictions that the world will either end or that we will experience some sort of catastrophic event.

With so much fear and uncertainty surrounding "What will happen in 2012?", we decided to ask Eloheim for their perspective.

In this 57 page book, Eloheim explains how we can use the energies of "2012" for our spiritual growth and answers the following questions:

What did the Mayans know about 2012 and why does their calendar end in December of 2012?; Why did the Hopi point to 2012 and say any chance at salvation is now useless as we have gone too far?; Why is there so much fear about 2012?

Isn't it pretty likely there will be one or more disasters in the future?; Is it true that the Earth's population will be reduced to 500 million?; Will Jesus reappear in 2012?; Will aliens rescue the surviving population like a modern Noah's ark?; Are aliens already here?; Is the Earth going to be like a cell dividing in two—people who ascend going with the new Earth and the others staying behind thinking the rest are dead or gone?

Will there be a nuclear war or will the Earth be hit by an asteroid causing an ice age?; Are pole shifts occurring that may cause chaos in 2012? How about solar flares and problems related to that causing Earth disturbances?; Is it true that a civilization will emerge from middle Earth in 2012?; Is overpopulation going to cause a disaster in 2012?

We learn by crisis. Does it appear that we're getting it or do we need bigger and bigger crises to move ahead?; Regarding 2012, are there any safe areas?; If it's true that everyone is going to ascend anyway, what's the point in all the work that we're doing?; How can I deal with my fear and anxiety regarding 2012? Is there anything I should do to prepare for it?; What will happen after 2012?

The book also contains four of Eloheim's tools for spiritual growth: Point fingers; What's in your lap?; What is true now?; and You to you. Additionally, there are 62 definitions of terms and concepts including: ascension, creating your reality, consciousness-based operating system, energetics, ensoulment, free will, Homo spiritus, shadow, soul's perspective, transformation, vibration, and your internal world creates your external experience.

The book closes with information about Eloheim and The Council and a description of the channeling process.

Use the energy of 2012 to facilitate your personal growth!

—*Eloheim*

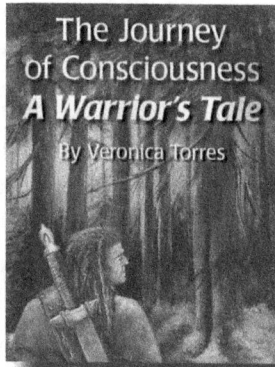

The Journey of Consciousness, A Warrior's Tale

"This entire story is to help you know who you are."

This "fairy tale for grown-ups" follows the Warrior's journey as he encounters castles and kings, battles and beasties, while learning to live from an open heart. The Warrior explains how to live the truth of you, how to have a healthy relationship to authority figures, and how to be vulnerable and strong at the same time.

"Anything that is presenting itself to you is presenting itself to you for growth."

Filled with humor, sage advice, penetrating insight, and above all, profound support for your process, the Warrior's tale clarifies your spiritual path.

"Now, it's really fun to see the King when you stink. Why? Because

what you want the king to know is that you are not just a little pawn in his game to be manipulated to his benefit. When you go to see the king, whomever the king is in your world, take who you are with you, and if that means you drop mud on this perfect floor, well, there you are."

***

The Warrior is one of the seven Council members channeled by Veronica Torres. The Council's teachings focus on spiritual growth and the movement from the fear-based to the consciousness-based operating system. They specialize in offering specific tools which will facilitate your spiritual growth.

In addition to the Warrior's story, The Journey of Consciousness includes the following tools: Clarity vs. certainty; Feet under shoulders; How ridiculous does it have to get?; I don't know anything; Lay it down and walk away; Mad scientist; Neutral observation; "No" is a complete sentence; Point fingers; Preferences/judgments; Script holding/Script-holders; Strongest chakra; Vulnerability vs. weakness; What's in your lap?; What is true now?; Where am I lying to myself? "Wow!", not "why?", and You to you (comparing). It also includes 126 definitions of terms and concepts used in The Council's teachings.

***

"When you're facing your triggers, if you start to waiver in your courage, just imagine that we stand behind you. We stand there to show you that you don't have to fear that you are not enough. You can be afraid of the triggers, but don't be afraid that you're not enough. We will stand beside you in consciousness and courage any time you wish."

—*The Warrior*

***

Eloheim and The Council books are available online through major book retailers and by visiting eloheim.com/dlg/cart/index.php.

Praise for Ruins of Redemption

¡Qué interesantes poemas!
Oigo la música y el sentimiento de Lorca con un toque de Neruda en tu
poema "Una noche cualquiera". Verdaderamente bello. Tu poema
"Lluvia" es un aguacero que le falta clavos en el mundo concreto.
Muchas ideas, y pocas imágenes, pero me gusta la imagen del techo de
zinc. Tu poema "Lágrimas" tiene mucha pasión y emoción, pero también
le falta clavos en la vida real. Es más bien una oración que un poema.
Gracias por darme la oportunidad de leer tu exitoso trabajo.
¡Buena suerte!

What interesting poems!
I hear the music and the feeling of Lorca with a touch of Neruda in your
poem, "Una Noche Cualquiera." Truly beautiful. Your poem, "Lluvia" is a
downpour missing nails in the real world. Many ideas, and few pictures,
but I like the image of the tin roof . Your poem "Lágrimas" has a lot of
passion and emotion, but also lacks nails in real life . It's more like a
prayer than a poem.
Thank you for the opportunity to read your successful work.
Good luck!

Eddie Vega
Author of *Awake Now, Sailor*
www.eddievega.com